Seasons
In Upper Turkeyfoot
A Countryman's Journal
By
JEFF O'BRIEN

Lucid Press
Sausalito, California
1999

Seasons in Upper Turkeyfoot

©1999 Jeff O'Brien. All Rights Reserved
No portion of this book may be reproduced
or used in any form, or by any means, without
written permission of the publishers.

Printed in the United States of America

Library of Congress Cataloging-in-Publication Data
   Seasons in Upper Turkeyfoot: a Countryman's Journal/by Jeff O'Brien.
     p.   cm.
ISBN 0-9646184-3-5
1. Upper Turkeyfoot (Pa. : Township) --Social life and customs.
2. Country life--Pennsylvania--Upper Turkeyfoot (Township)
3. Seasons--Pennsylvania--Upper Turkeyfoot (Township)
4. Natural history--Pennsylvania--Upper Turkeyfoot (Township)
5. O'Brien, Jeff, 1945- . I. Title
F159.U68037 1999
974.8'79--dc21   99-33386
                                                        CIP

Cover design: Vince Valdes
Illustrations and photographs by Jeff O'Brien
Copy Editor: A. Ranney Johnson

Published by Lucid Press
10 Liberty Ship Way
Sausalito, California 94965

10 9 8 7 6 5 4 3 2 1

Contents

Spring   One to forty

Summer   Forty one to eighty four

Fall   Eighty five to one hundred twenty six

Winter   One hundred twenty seven to one hundred sixty six

About the Author

Jeff O'Brien is a syndicated newspaper columnist with more than 25 years experience as a sports writer, news editor, managing editor and magazine publisher who has chosen nature with its endless variety and moods as his venue. His faithful readers, who number more than a half million in Pennsylvania alone, have savored his words in essays, magazine articles and on National Public Radio. The recipient of over 40 state and national awards, (in the same year) he was named both best humorous and the best serious columnist by the National Newspaper Association. Be warned. Jeff O'Brien can be habit forming!

Acknowledgments

My effusive thanks to Bob Greenberg without whose kindly and generous help this book would not exist, and to Claire Huff for her support, intelligent advice, and hard work. I wish also to express my gratitude to the K.W. Saylor family and to the Terry and Peggy Ream family, particularly to their sons Mark and Danny, all of whom will be surprised to find themselves mentioned here. Their commitment to farming contributes much to the quality of my life. To Jerry and Joy Knepp, and to Mike and Margaret Flinn, I am grateful for their encouragement and unflagging friendship. Thanks also to Kelly O'Brien for taking time away from her own writing to help her father, and to Chad O'Brien for carrying on the name in these hills he loves at least as much as I do. And finally to my wife, Tracy, thank you for showing me the power of belief.

--J O'B

Introduction

Upper Turkeyfoot is a township in the Laurel Mountains of south-western Pennsylvania. Some might call it south-central;. No one who lives here is sure how to describe it exactly. That suits us just fine. If these wooded hills and valleys are hard to locate, we'd like to keep it that way. We watch what's happening in the broader world, and we're not sure change is always the best thing.

The Laurel Mountains are among the oldest mountains on earth and showing their age, the peaks worn long ago to rounded ridges. Yes, there is a Lower Turkeyfoot. Upper and Lower combine to form the Turkeyfoot Valley. And, yes, wild turkeys thrive here. Most warm evenings I hear them clucking in their roosts.

The Turkeyfoot region gets its name from the confluence of three streams in the shape of a turkey's foot. A 20-year old George Washington referred to it as "Turkey Foot" on a map he drew of his expedition into the wilderness in 1752.

Where I live has always been more important to me than what I do. Place defines me. As a young man, I realized I must live in the country if I were to have any chance at contentment. That conviction, which I still hold, led me to accept a minimum wage job at a small newspaper in these mountains. I put down $5 "hand money" on a derelict farmhouse and a few acres of land. Squirrels gnawed in the attic, groundhogs in the cellar. More than 25 years later, I still find each day a wonder.

I did the work myself, having no money and therefore no choice. This old homestead may not be much to look at, yet it is my own.

Sitting in my living room, it is as if I can look straight up through the pine tree that leans over the roof and know that the Big Dipper is standing on its handle above the old silo. I know every hummock and swale in the land itself. I know where the grouse feed and where the rain will collect at the back of the field. I know where the Maypoles will sprout and the wild bergamot bloom. I have place wisdom.

Living in Upper Turkeyfoot does not mean I can escape the inevitable ravages of existence. But when they come, I always have the shadowed wood, the unmowed field, the open sky. The natural world sustains me. Sometimes I think this might be as close as I will ever come to paradise. Other times, I'm sure of it.

May this book pass along some small portion of that.

--Jeff O'Brien

Spring

Spring Training

Two young men lie in the outfield sunning themselves like old dogs.

It is 42 degrees, and the ground is still frozen beneath the dead grass. Yet there they lie, propped on their elbows, coatless, ballcaps backwards, teenagers.

I am returning from the woods where I sat against an oak and considered existence, where brittle leaves clattered above me and crows echoed deep in the valley as the sun swung westward and the hills softened in the blue distance.

I climb the bank and cross the infield. The boy has come to visit. This ballfield I built for him and his sister a decade ago. I wave.

Matt is there. Matt lives back the road, yet I am nearly upon them before I know him. He has grown tall and dark-haired in the years since my son went to live over the hill with his mother.

The boy's car is parked wet and gleaming beside the stable. I will put away the bucket and hose later. For now, I offer to make them each a couple of chili dogs. They accept with enthusiasm. Lying on the frozen ground makes a fellow hungry.

While I thaw chili sauce, they stride off into the woods to check out their old fort in the big rocks. I bury pink tubes of pulverized poultry parts in mustard and sauce, slip a flagon of root beer into my coat pocket, and find them on the gravel in front of the garage tossing stones into air and whacking them into the cornfield with the broken shovel handles I keep there for that very purpose.

We eat standing. "Delicious," Matt says. He has always been polite.

Into the garage I go and reappear with a ball and three gloves.

"All right!" the boy says.

"Male bonding!" Matt says.

"You bet!" I say.

We trot onto the field, form a triangle, and play catch. Nothing too hard. It is, after all, February.

A game is created, as always. Rules are established, amended.

"No moving," the boy says.

"Yeah," Matt says. "Except you can take one step. You can pivot, like in basketball."

"Yeah," I say. "And if you lift your pivot foot you have to put your finger in your nose and cluck like a chicken."

"Yeah!"

"Yeah!"

Strategy develops: lobs, grounders, in-between hops, projectiles just out of reach, rocket shots high into the sun, look one way and throw another. We love this, we males.

Raised on a hill overrun by boys, I spent the days of my youth with contests involving a ball. Home from school, change your clothes, out the door, pick up sides, play 'til dark.

In summer the game would continue through supper, brothers leaving when called and returning in minutes. In winter we'd shovel snow off Mr. Waters' driveway (the only paved one with a hoop) and wear our mothers' rubber kitchen gloves to ward off frostbite.

Sometimes a Dad would appear, beg for the ball, show a little of the old flash, strut for a second, then vanish once more into the warmth and the responsibility.

So here we are, a high school sophomore, a senior, and a middle-aged transcendentalist, all grunting and lunging and laughing and sprawling and clucking on this still-frozen field and the dead grass as if it were July.

"Come on!" the boy yells at Matt. "You're six-foot-tall. Stretch those long legs!" I, they discover, am particularly gifted at imitating a hen laying an egg.

I move as under a stronger gravity than these boys. My legs are leaden. The ball flies true enough from my hand, but it has no life, no pop when it hits the mitt. And how I must concentrate on the casual bullets fired by my son, how I must focus all my degenerating faculties on the elliptical blur that forces me to sacrifice my hand in order to save my organs.

My face burns from the sun and the wind. My ears sting from the cold. My shoulder throbs. My knees ache. My hand is surely broken. I am a happy man. Forget the calendar. It is spring.

March Unplugged

The sun has crossed the equator again and is headed our way.

We open the windows to let in the breezes and let out the flies and the ladybugs. We stand in the yard with our shirts open and our pantlegs pulled up, exposing to the purifying light the things that have been growing under our clothes all winter. We do some thinking about renewal.

The garage roof needs painting, and the pond needs dredging. The cellar needs cleaning, and the windows need glazing. This old place, it seems, would collapse around us if we let it.

But for now we are content to stand and look out across the fields toward the wooded hills. This is a rare moment. It is quiet. No cars on the road. No tractor in the field. No planes in the sky.

Quiet moments such as this are more and more difficult to come by. Even here in Upper Turkeyfoot it is a treat to escape the cacophony of men and their engines, unplugged.

Yet such moments of uninterrupted solitude are necessary, we think, if we are to renew ourselves.

Out from under roof, standing in the open air, seeing as far as our eyes can see, our senses liberated, with the quiet and the wind roaring in our ears, we soar.

In this solitude, the problem of existence is simplified. We feel the elevation of spirit we find in little else, not in personal triumph, nor financial gain, nor in anything offered by man or his society.

We explore the higher latitudes. This is what the poet called the winged life. Our reward is neither fame nor fortune, but what already exists in the soul, a freshness shared by hawks and trees.

We know what is really important. We value, once more, the little things in life, the midges dancing in the light, the grass growing under our feet. We cherish the present.

Our eyes are open, our world intact. Evidence of ancient cycles surrounds us. Buds swell on the lilacs and maples. The birds return. Sap flows. Soon in the woods, fiddleheads will unroll and Maypoles will colonize the loam. Nature is confident.

Loren Eiseley wrote that there exists "an old contract never broken till man began to interfere with wild things, that nature, in degree, is steadfast and continuous."

Standing in the yard with the earth awakening around us, we understand the promise.

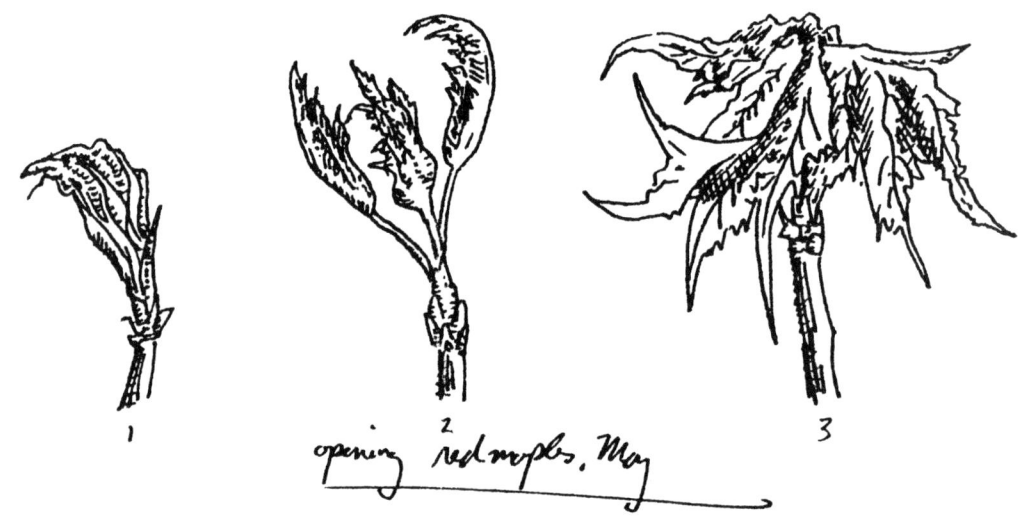

Lady Bugs, Maple Sugar

Tapped sugar maples this week. Old timers will tell you it's time when the days turn bright and sharp, and the nights cold and starry.

I drilled a few holes in the big sugars near the old camp. The bit came out wet, and a rivulet of sugar water darkened the bark before I could tap in the spile and hang the bucket. Oldtimers are almost always right.

Yet now there's another way to know. Now, when the Asian Lady Beetles mass inside my window, its time to cut spiles.

Spiles are spouts. You can buy them in the kind of hardware store with floorboards, or you can cut them from elderberry bushes, as I do, and hollow out the pith.

Asian Lady Beetles are our little orange and tan friends who have recently taken up permanent residency in Pennsylvania. We spend the winters together now, the beetles and me, ever since they first showed up in Upper Turkeyfoot in 1993.

Don't panic. These are good bugs, entomologists will tell you. Entomologists are educated persons who teach at universities or work for the state and answer the phone when you call the Department of Agriculture and say, "What's with all the bugs on my windows?"

Lady beetles, you see, eat aphids. Aphids are — well, you've seen Nature. Even better, these Ladybugs also eat a pest that attacks Christmas trees. Gauging by the beetle husks piling up on my window sills, I might just plant the field in spruces. Given my innate ability to generate capital, my Christmas trees should reach maturity just in time for North America to be taken over by Hasballa or Jehova's Witnesses or some such anti-Holidays crowd.

During the Middle Ages, ladybugs rid grapevines of aphids, saving the wine crop. Overcome with joy (this calls for a toast!), folks dedicated the beetles to "Our Lady," hence their common name.

The Asian variety came ashore in New Orleans in 1989 and has spread rapidly northward. Their tendency to aggregate makes them obvious as as they seek shelter over winter. They now compete for lodging in my house with me and the wife and the dogs and the cluster flies and the attic squirrels and the cellar mice and the freaky, musk-exuding, Western conifer seed bugs that turn their heads to watch me and take flight if they see me coming with a tissue.

These guys, too, are latecomers and harmless, I'm told; I just don't like being stared at.

"Whadyou lookin' at Leptoglossus Occidentalis? You got a problem?"

So, spring begins. The sap rises and falls. My buckets fill. I vacuum the carcasses from the sills. I'm happy to be tapping maples, because I needed to get out more. The beetles, quite frankly, were giving me the heebie-jeebies.

I'm up late. Countless times during the night I snap on the lamp and read a few pages. I keep everything handy — books, notepad, pencils, water glass, Cheese Nips. Often I fall asleep with the light on. They seem to like the light. Or maybe it's the Cheese Nips. Either way, they aggregate around my head. Sometimes one gets under the quilt, and I feel it crawling on my thigh.

"Just nerves," I'll tell myself and try to sleep, reasonably sure the bed is devoid of pasturing aphids. But it only takes once. Only once do you need to reach down and find a beetle on your leg, and you are forever traumatized. Every lint ball, every Cheese Nip crumb grows six legs and mandibles and an ovipositor, and you're sure you've got larvae feeding on your flesh beneath your skin. Sure, you've seen Nature, but you've seen Alien, too.

The water glass I have kept covered ever since, half asleep, I spit one across the room. They thirst. More than once I've awakened to one drinking from the corner of my eye. It freaks me out, beneficial or not. I'd be a lot happier if I had a wine supply to save.

Meanwhile, I've been checking my records. The 17-years locusts will be back in 1999. Perfect. Those red-eyed whirrers should send the Millennial Prophets of Doom over the edge.

And that's not all. the Asian Long-Horned Beetle has been spotted killing Norway maples in Brooklyn. In Brooklyn when you cut down a tree in the backyard, you have to carry it through the house to load it on the truck.

The Asian Long-Horned Beetle is black-and-white and bigger than a Junebug. It drills holes in the trees. If I were to awaken in the middle of the night and see one drinking from the corner of my eye, it would look as big as a Holstein.

So, watch out.

I'm going out now to walk on the snow crust and empty my buckets in moonlight. Then I'm going to bed and try not to think about it. As a gesture of peace, I think I'll scatter Cheese Nips in the field. Harmony with nature sometimes takes a little work.

Ramps Ruin Big Plans

Big plans tonight. O'Brien and the wife are going out.

Pizza and a movie: "Secrets and Lies." Mushrooms and sausage. They do this a lot, favoring, as they do, thick crust and a big screen and each other.

A follower of current events (as we all are whether we want to be not), O'Brien has come up with a name for this evening's event. He calls it a "Doe Date."

While he congratulates himself on his cleverness, he also feels compelled to explain that this is how Heaven's Gate cult members spent their evening after videotaping their farewells.

Before leaving for the next level of existence, they filled their containers with $417.27 worth of pizza. Then they watched "Secrets and Lies" and drank $75 worth of soda.

O'Brien is amazed he knows this. He figured he already knew more than he cared to about Marshall Applewhite and his dreamy followers. But as soon as he signed on, there it was on the screen, injected into his brain through his eyeballs, pizza and a movie and seven quarts of Starbuck's Java Chocolate Chip ice cream in the freezer.

He signs off, checks his pocket watch, and, giving the stem a wind, decides he has time for a walk in the woods before his big night out.

He visits the woodland pond and adds his bootprints to the deer tracks in the black mud. Heavy ripples radiate from under a poplar limb. Something strong and cold and otherworldly has fled to the safety of the deep.

Waterstriders scoot about near the water's edge. A drying wind sends last season's leaves clattering along the bank. High above the pond and reflected on the surface with the sky and a cloud, the maples bloom.

All of this pleases him. But what excites him most are the fresh colonies of green leaves sprouting from the bank. The ramps are up.

Ramps are one of the first edible plants of spring. Two or three broad leaves open from a purple sheath. The stem is white and soft, and the real treat lies just beneath the loam, the tender bulb, sweet and pungent, strong enough to isolate you among the uninitiated.

Ramps are wild leeks. They contain the same benefits as fresh garlic (and the same odor), and have been used over the centuries as a folk remedy for everything from headaches to cancer.

Feasting on ramps is a rite of spring in these mountains. In West Virginia, the appearance of ramps is cause for celebration. They conduct festivals. Years ago, an enterprising old editor had the scent chemically duplicated and mixed with his ink to remind native readers who had moved away. The mail stunk.

O'Brien likes that kind of thinking, and believes it worthy of recognition. A plaque or something. What that wizened editor got was a stern warning from the U. S. Postal Service.

So, O'Brien, folksy and proud of it, eats a ramp. He pulls up another and takes it home for his wife. She declines. Town girl.

"I love you," she says. "But you need a mint."

O'Brien showers, brushes, gargles, talcs, colognes. It helps not. The only real antidote for ramps is to get everybody nearby to eat them, too. That, and a couple of cases.

Pariah though he may be, O'Brien is happy. He reeks.

But the night, he realizes, may not be as big as he had envisioned.

Pure Listening

*"The pre-dawn pact lasts only as long as darkness humbles the arrogant.
It would seem as if the sun were responsible for the daily
retreat of reticence from the world
—Aldo Leopold, "Sand County Almanac."*
* * *

A scrape in the dark, and sulphur glows like a tracer on the striker.

The match hisses into flame, transfers its combustion to the candle wick, and the room fills with shape and shadow. Darkness, expelled from the cabin, presses its face against the glass.

At 4 a.m., there is no sign of morning here in the foggy wood, but light enough to see the trunks of trees gathered 'round in the translucent mist like old friends come to comfort and console.

Steam rising from your cup, you watch the day begin.

Listen. Such peace the day knows not; —your breathing is the loudest sound. Hear the hum of your existence.

Thrill at a snarl in the woooded depths. A racoon perhaps? A mink or great-horned owl, their murders interrupted? You know not, for this is a strange time, a time for creatures of the sun, like men, to sleep and dream.

By 5 a.m., when cardinals sing, there is light enough collected on the page to write. Species by species, the chorus builds as damp night air creeps down the slope before the advance of morning, the day announced by music and the drip of dew. Listen.

Shh. Hear, beyond the hill, the sigh of tires upon the road; man joins the song.

The mist recedes, beat back by light that surrounds you as if the sun rose from your brow, as if you were the center of the universe. Look, now--Maypoles reaching for the light, violets, closed against the night, open. Crows take flight.

Water boils on the stove. Put down your pen. The day is here. Tend to the trivialities of living.

white pine

House Numbers

O'Brien gets his new 911 address. He scowls.

It is one of the few pieces of mail he actually opens without just ripping it in half and chucking it in the burn bag. He has been waiting for this moment. He knew it was coming. Ambulance drivers must find their way, after all. Still the house number doesn't please him.

He used to be RD 1. Now he's 522 Handwerk Road and, oh, it sounds so much more urbane. A number to remember. More forms to complete.

The notice he places on the kitchen table on the pile with all the other statements and invoices and compellations. O'Brien subscribes to the Avalanche Principle: When the stack grows so high that it slides onto the linoleum, he takes care of business.

Years ago, it seems, municipal officials had started naming every road in the county. In the country, many of the roads have been locally known for generations by the farms to which they led--Ream Road, Wagner Road, McGuire Road.

But now, driving down the hard two-lane that is the main north-south artery through these hills, you can tell which roads have been developed by the new green signs. Parceling has led to names like Pineview or Briarpatch or Maple Ridge Heights. Very cute.

O'Brien likes the old names better. Poverty Hollow is one. Handwerk is another. He was going to suggest to the township supervisors that they name his road "RD 1" so he could use up all those stickers from charitable organizations to which he can no longer afford to contribute. But they never asked him.

Still, Handwerk is fine. A good German name. They worked hard here, and a green sign is a small tribute.

Yet O'Brien is disturbed by the attached regulations and enforcements. Along with the new address are instructions for mounting the numbers on his house. If he refuses, he will be fined $300 a day. This gets his Irish up. He is summarily offended.

O'Brien, you see, is like the shipwrecked Irishman washed up on an isolated island. A native appears and gives him water, saving him.

"Do you have a government?" asks the Irishman.

"We do," says the native.

"I'm against it," says the Irishman.

Country people are an independent lot. We don't like being told what to do, even when it is for our own good. Never mind that if I were to call the local volunteers, they would know where I live by my name alone. I am required to nail numbers on my house.

First it's numbers nailed on your house, then it's numbers tattooed on your forehead. (O'Brien doesn't really believe it will lead to that. He's just worked up. To blame could be the suggestion that the numbers be fluorescent.)

O'Brien and his neighbors have just gotten used to the idea of a building code. They still grumble about having to buy a permit to patch their roofs to keep the rain from coming in, and now this. Next thing, they'll be regulating the size of satellite dishes and their proximity to derelict Impalas, not that O'Brien has either, but he believes in civil liberty.

A neighboring county has lowered the penalty to $25. The theory is they won't feel as bad about fining folks. Life brims with irony.

Understand, O'Brien is no subversive. He finds a loophole. His house is more than 50 feet from the road—near enough for the dust raised by ATVs to pass through his screens, but far enough to exempt him from numbers on the siding.

All he has to do is display the number close to the road. He knows a perfect locust post amid the rosebushes. He goes looking for a crayon. He is a law-abiding man.

A Proper Distance

At the edge of the field I sit with my back against the split rail fence, looking out from under the bill of my cap and across my life. The long view calms me.

I am far enough away to take in the sweep of hilltop and treeline, the alternating swaths of corn stubble, the greening alfalfa, the drift of blue-bottomed clouds.

Here in the sunlight and birdsong, last week's snowfall seems remote. I read it now in my journal, feeling one winter closer to my last.

Into the woods I went to watch it fall on the leafmat, the landings accumulating into a soft hiss in the woods, a steady sibilance that became a chorus for the breathing of the wind. By lunchtime it had turned to sleet, the hiss rising from the ground into the treetops. By afternoon it fell as porcelain beads, bouncing off my thighs as I ran on the wet road, robins fleeing before me.

Forgive my rambling. Such days as this set me off.

A crow caws at me. Mourning doves coo in the pines that surround the house seen across the gleaming field, a two-story frame built on locust logs laid on a fieldstone foundation.

Though I have lived here 25 years, it seems not mine, not from this distance. It could be argued that the house belongs to the bank, but the mortgage will be paid in a few years. When that day comes, I will, no doubt, conduct the traditional fiery ceremony, and I will think, "Mine, at last."

Yet from this distance I can see at the edge of the yard the last furrow of the old plowing line. At my back runs a row of stone picked from this field by generations. Arrowheads — I have found one — lie beneath the grass. The house itself, its timbers cut from this very hilltop and bearing the gashes of adzes, is no more mine than the land, or the sky. I am the current resident, no more, no less.

My presence is temporary. I am far enough away to know it. Though I have worked for 25 years to build the garage and the stable and the coop, to keep the field mowed and the roof patched, all would collapse in the blink of an eye after my death, without another caretaker.

No more lasting am I than the snow of last week.

Yet it is enough to feel the moment, to listen to the bullfrogs groan. The toads sang today as if for the first time. I am far enough away to think it important.

Far enough away am I to watch the wind approach through the ruddy tops of blooming maples. Far enough away to see the swifts return. Far enough away to watch the distant hills, blue with mist, rise to meet the sun. Far enough away to feel the earth roll, and all of us with it — me beneath the boughs here against the split rail, the midges spinning in low sunlight, the crow in the treetops behind me, you with this book in your hand, all of us rolling with it, all of us made of the stuff of the universe, and only the spheres surviving.

Too introspective, this, for a newspaper column, even so close to Earth Day. (Accused of that before, I plead guilty.) Yet these thoughts are commonplace.

Men and women have sensed this connectedness as far back as we can tell. All it takes is the proper distance, be it alone on the mountaintop, or wandering in the desert, or standing on the moon. It is a knowledge rediscovered in solitude, a wisdom gained in silence.

Far enough away, we know the truth. May we act accordingly.

Born in the Typewriter

This old manual typewriter clacks away, and the words march across the page (ding!) a letter at a time. I have reclaimed it from the mouse.

The mouse has relocated. I can hear her setting up house on the other side of the cabin, shredding paper inside the Coleman stove, nipping it into crescents like the bits I blew out of these keys.

We have reached an understanding, the mouse and me. Now I can work, and she can feed her babies—hungry little urchins with powers of suction great enough to hold fast while Momma scuttled down the leg of the desk and raced behind the woodstove, dragging her children along the wall to hide in the farthest corner of the room, behind the stormdoor window stored there for the summer.

She watched me through the glass, facing a dilemma.

Panting from her escape, she pulled her pups closer to her, stroking their coats with the pink pads of her white feet. Only two pups. Children were lost.

I had opened the desk door, swung out the spring-loaded typewriter shelf, uncovered the machine, and discovered it packed with pink insulation and shredded paper. I had removed most of it when I saw it move.

I knelt on the pine floor and looked under the typewriter. She looked back at me, whiskers shivering, eyeball to eyeball, a foot apart. That's when I saw the young ones suckling, sleek and gray with white bellies, their eyes beginning to open. Almost three weeks old, I'd say.

When Momma made her move, two pups lost their grip on the shelf support under the desk. I pushed them off with a ruler and into my hand. They chirped like birds. I heard Momma coming back.

The white-footed mouse is the most common rodent in Pennsylvania. Also called the wood mouse or the field mouse, it looks like the deer mouse, except its tail lacks the white tuft at the end.

I don't mind mice in the cabin. They are neat animals, and besides, I couldn't keep them out if I tried.

After we stared at each other for a few minutes, this one judged me no immediate threat and took to cleaning her face just as a cat does, licking its feet and grooming its fur and whiskers. And once I saw her run the floor and the stones, shielding the woodstove and up the wall and invisibly above the ceiling to reappear at an opening over the bed, I realized this was at least as much her domain as mine. She is the permanent resident; I am the visitor.

Like the deer mouse, the white-footed mouse forms the base of the vertebrate food chain. Its predators are many. I am not among them. It consumes about 30 per cent of its body weight in food per day.

I figured it out. For me, that would amount to three gallons of milk and 35 boxes of Cheese Nips a day. But white-footed mice eat mostly insects, seeds, and caterpillars. They play a key role in the control of gypsy moths.

So I let them be. Babies born in April can have babies of their own by July. A female can have four litters a season, but few of them live so long.

Mice learn quickly. I read that in one office building they learned to run to the wastebaskets for scraps at the sound of the lunch bell. I might try that, maybe with a whistle. If it works, I could become locally famous as the The Pied Piper of Upper Turkeyfoot.

Momma returned alone to the desk and gave me another lookover. Then off she went to move her two babies from behind the glass. She carried them in her mouth by the scruff of the necks and wasted no time in locating another nest site in the Coleman stove.

I retrieved the old nest from the trash, put it in the stove and laid the lost pups in the fiberglass. They cleaned their faces, neatness bred in the bone. I watched as she found them. She gave me another look and a sniff, sticking her nose through the chrome rack, then scooted under the fluff and yanked her children to safety from below.

I went back to writing this column. She came back twice to the desk. Mice probably can't count, and she was just making sure. At least that's what I'm guessing. You can't read too much into things.

Careful Praise of Beauty

The words we use define us.

The beauty of this world streams around us without end —"all things beautiful in their time," as we read in Ecclesiastes. What changes is how we describe it.

Today, working under a great fleet of speeding clouds with flat, gray bottoms, watching continents of shade sweep across the hills and the shivering grass, I wonder how best to say what I feel, how to write it — and this isn't it, but life is short, and to the making of newspaper columns there is no end.

If that sounds a bit biblical, well, I have always been influenced most by what I read last. Today my writing is flowery, though I prefer a leaner style, limiting the adjectives and adverbs and letting the verbs flex their muscles. But April is a flowery month, so I gush.

In town, everybody exclaims upon the weather, for that is the first of just two topics each of us cares about the same. We are all of this earth with no escape but one, and therein lies the second.

Being thrifty as well as wordy, a sale compels me to drive to the feed mill. They are going out of business. This is dairy country, and farmers are struggling. I load the truck (dog food and sunflower seed are 40 per cent off), and I think about the land.

Farming has always been hard work. Now, I hear, it is barely profitable, if at all. Little wonder, then, that the countryside is dotted with derelict barns.

Lately I have seen a lot of log trucks on the road. More timber is being cut than I can remember. Coasting behind the trucks, waiting for a chance to pass, I notice the diameters are smaller than they used to be. I have no facts to back this up. Just observations from the hills.

Serious talk, this, as we load the pickup. Then the feed mill man smiles and wishes me well and tells me to enjoy this beautiful day.

So, people — as well as hills, and cloud shadows, and returning birds, and awakening frogs, and gleaming grass — people, too, add to the quality of the day.

When they do, I'd like to tell them so. But you have to watch your words.

A man can't just go around firing off compliments. He would be considered a bit touched. It is true, of course, that "a cheerful heart is good medicine," but such unusual behavior is likely to invite a mugging, or end in litigation. At the very least, it raises suspicion.

I offer a domestic example. You may recognize the conversation. My wife dresses for town. She is no primper, but wants to look businesslike.

"How do I look?" she asks.

"You look great," I say.

"You didn't even look at me," she says.

"I did," I say. "You look terrific."

"I don't," she says.

"You do," I say.

"You're just saying that," she says.

My guess is that this conversation takes place in hundreds of millions of households all over the world. Searching for better words, I turn to The Song of Solomon, lyrical passages about love and marriage. Perhaps I should try this:

"Your hair is like a flock of goats, moving down the slopes of Gilead."

That is sure to get a reaction. Or, I could try:

"Your teeth are like a flock of shorn ewes."

Her childhood orthodontist could use that on his signboard.

Remember, this was high praise thousands of years ago, professions of love by a wise king in a herding society. But in America, at the end of the Twentieth Century, I doubt you could sweep a girl off her feet with:

"Your nose is like a tower of Lebanon, overlooking Damascus."

If my wife were, say, a woman of the pampas, she might be impressed. But she is a Western Pennsylvania girl, so my search for metaphor must continue.

I mean no disrespect. I only mean to illustrate how difficult it is to say what you mean, and to be understood, and how rare that is.

So we talk about the weather, a safe subject, but we mean so much more.

Seeing in Spring Rain

Lightning shakes the house.

It snaps and booms. The earth shudders. That was close.

We had no warning. No rising wind. No distant thunder rolling over ridges of the Allegheny front. No yellow, eerie calm that in summer tells the countryman to prop the barn doors closed.

We are not harmed, only startled. In spring the lightning strikes unannounced, as if we lived at the origin of storms.

That is easy to believe if we leave the shelter of the house and stand in the rain with the earth going green around us. Are we not, each of us, the center of our own reality? Let philosophers and prophets determine what is real and what imagined. The two could be the same for all we know, drunk on ozone and verse. A walk will clear our heads.

The temperature has dropped 10 degrees in minutes. The rain began as pattering on the roof, then set the can to ringing under the gutter. Now it marches over the land, and for the first time this year we hear the susurrating leaves, tender though they be, the great crowns bowing, harps for wind.

How do I see so much, you ask? The question surprises me, for I know I see so little and miss so much more. What I see in nature is only the obvious, there for all who would look. Anyone can do it. You need only be still and alert and let nature do its work.

Rilke called this, "the outer standstill and the inner movement."

Let us go then in the rain, the drops fringing our hoods, but seen only against the trees and ground and invisible against the sky which they contain.

Let us cultivate our capacity for stillness, for solitary contemplation. A priest once told me this was prayer. The trajectory is similar. So be it.

We become as wet as trees, the water shining on the backs of our hands, soaking into our pantlegs.

We stop to examine the progress of the leaves, the oaks still folded and in down, the maples expanding over their swelling keys, the fruit of elms hanging in clusters.

Everywhere we look, pale petals litter the ground, petals of apple and choke cherry and plum gone wild.

There is a delicacy to the woods that lasts but a few days — the leaves in their infancy, Maypoles and violets mobbing in the light, the smallest plants and saplings greening first, the vegetable world lunging toward the sun before the canopy of the big trees shades the loam.

This is a time too often missed, occupied as we become with our shabby lives; too often it is summer suddenly.

"Life is a spell so exquisite that everything tries to break it," Emily Dickinson wrote.

We stoop to lift the flap of a solitary jack-in-the-pulpit, the spadix firm in its striped canopy. No beauty but in things, the poet Williams said. We understand it better now.

We only need to stop. We only need to look.

Death of an Old Man

Life is full of death.

O'Brien has been thinking lately. He does so while reveling in the chores of a bright morning. It is that kind of day, in late April when you are convinced, at last, that the snow is gone.

He sharpens the maul, firm strokes with the file. He splits wood. He straightens the log pile, and the scurry of something dark does not startle him. He is preoccupied with the Big Question.

The day is right for working — cool and calm, a T-shirt day if you keep your muscles flexing — enriched by birdsong, and isles of clouds, and sweat on the brow.

An old man has died.

O'Brien loved him, loved him for his honesty, for his strength of spirit, for his country ways.

He swings the maul. Thunk. Cherry cleaved, the halves fly and drop in the growing grass.

"Feel better," O'Brien had said to him last winter. He sat in his recliner, recovering from the flu, his cane at his side as it had been since his stroke, the TV so loud you had to shout.

"If I don't," the old man said, the body wearing out but not the spirit, "come see me up Sharp's."

Sharp's is the funeral home in the small town nearest the family farm.

"I've lived a good life," he said. And he had. "I'm ready."

Sharp's it was to be.

O'Brien swings the maul, thunk, and thinks of the gathering: the children, white-haired and stricken; the grandchildren, somber and strong, the spirit multiplied; some a bit removed, too young to know, but learning. He thinks of the great-grandchildren, the toddlers and the babes-in-arms and the hope they hold for all.

He swings the maul, and wonders, will he be as strong at his own end? Thunk. Will he know when it is time to refuse treatment? Thunk. Will he arrange his affairs as surely and with as much courage, conviction, and consideration?

The maul jams. A steel wedge he drives into the log with a sledge. Morphine can be a blessing at the end, he thinks. The echo rings in the woods.

He stacks firewood, puts on his shirt, and drives to town for supplies — gas in the cans for the mower, calcium in bags for the dusty road, bar oil for the chainsaw, and maybe, if the mood strikes him, some pots of geraniums for the stone planter that caps the old well.

He takes the Chickentown Road to town. Driving with the window down and his elbow out (a treat in April), this rolling, winding, blacktopped, two-lane provides pictures as he passes, a sort of slide show, fragments of spring in the countryside.

Jeans filled with wind on clotheslines in backyards, sheets as brilliant and billowing as sails.

Goldfinches in their summer plumage on dried thistle.

Holsteins in parallel, grazing among dandelions, their muzzles in the grass; turned out for the first time, their milk will be strong tonight.

An old man in a straw hat with his sleeves rolled stoops in the garden with a child, their heads together.

Flashing flights of pigeons above silos, their shadows racing up the barn siding.

Cabbage moths and daffodils and wisps of color in the budding woods.

Yes, life is full of death. Yes, people make mistakes. Fear for the future, regret for the past — they age us, embitter us. Yet we cherish life because it is astonishingly beautiful, moment by moment. Know the present and be grateful. Joy exists. Hold fast.

Striders and Snakes

Another cold rain walks across the field. In town, buying mower parts and onion sets, folks complain. Another freeze expected tonight. Everything's behind. The fruit crop is ruined.

But we who love the natural world see such days as gifts. Let it come slowly, we think.

The weather toys with us, the sun burning the tops of our ears one moment, the snow surprising us the next.

Nature reminds us that change is constant. We know that, of course, yet all it takes is a few minutes of warmth to convince us life is forever balmy. We believe in promises.

We have not seen the juncos since the end of April, and we expect an end to frost. Yet we love the pace of spring this year. Let the hylas join the sunset chorus one voice at a time.

Standing by the pond, I called my daughter this week. She lives in Philadelphia. Her machine answered as always. I said nothing. The peepers left the message. She picked up as I guessed she would.

"Aw," she said. "Aw, Dad." She misses Upper Turkeyfoot more than she can admit.

Water draws me to it, free-flowing and full of life. A spring runs through the yard and spills into the pond. Waterstriders row about on the surface, searching for a meal. Their feet dimple water, the pads of their feet bending the surface but not breaking it.

They row with their middle legs, steer with their back legs (like rudders), and search for prey with their front legs, sensitive to vibrations from insects trapped in the packed molecules of surface tension.

I read that you can call water striders by imitating the flailings of, say, a fallen moth. I find two small sticks, put one in the water, and rub the other across it like a bow on a cello.

To my delight, hungry striders come a-rowing, even against the strong wind that continually blows them back.

This little trick I learned from a book of nature activities for children. Full of small amazements — some familiar like throwing a stone in the direction of a bat to watch it follow the arc, and some not so familiar like a thunderstorm is headed your way if the lightning is white, but not if it is yellow or orange — it is proof that the astonishments of childhood surround us our whole lives if we take the time to notice.

Walk with me up along the spring, expecting salamanders in the sudden sun. We find snakes.

Garter snakes in a knot, they do not startle us for we have seen them from far enough away. Just emerged from their dens, they lie warming themselves beside the water in a happy entanglement, their scales shining, glorying in the bright morning after a freezing night.

The eastern garter snake is a good neighbor. They eat mostly earthworms which they find near water. The last to hibernate in the fall and the first to come out in the spring, they will meet a friendly advance halfway.

"Easily tamed," we read in Comstock. But why would we do that. We like them wild. May they remain wary; not everyone who crosses this yard shares our acceptance of its inhabitants.

The snakes raise their gleaming heads and study us, their black-forked, scarlet tongues waggling to catch our scent. Brown with a yellow stripe down their back and with lighter sides, they have kind eyes.

The mailman stops. A neighbor haloos as he opens his box. When we look back, the snakes have dispersed, moving off under dandelions. The sun heats the backs of our necks. We wish them a pleasant summer. May it come slowly.

Town Going Rolex

Put on my town clothes yesterday and went.

I try to look respectable when I go to town. I even hosed the mud off the pickup.

I go to town twice a month whether I need to or not. It's good practice, saying hello and commiserating about the weather and all. Never know when I may have to abandon my asceticism and go back into the publishing business. A fellow needs to stay in practice, smiling and joshing and closing. Town is good for that.

I bought skim milk and crackers for me, rat poison and flypaper for the vermin, cracked corn and sunflower seed for the birds, and pellets and pig's ear jerky for the dogs, — you know — provisions. Plus, I bought 40 dollars at the ATM. That cost me fifty cents.

I visited the bank, and the market and the hardware store. I got what I needed, and I enjoyed the small talk. Best of all, I walked down the sidewalks in the sunshine, waving to old acquaintances on the other side of the street.

The chimney swifts are back, swirling above the post office. Maybe it was just one of those first, warm afternoons of spring, but this place is starting to feel like a real town again. Perhaps, after all, it has survived the opening of the Wal-Mart and the other "superstores" out where the big roads intersect. I see work being done on a few empty storefronts, and it lifts my spirits.

I also bought a battery for my watch. Haven't worn a watch much since I left academe to return to Upper Turkeyfoot. Picked it up when I was dusting the dresser the other day and noticed it had stopped. This pleased me, the way I live now.

Now, when I must know the exact time, I carry a wind-up in my pocket. It's been through the washer and the dryer, but I pried off the back, hung it from a string above the wood stove, and it works fine. Sometimes, when the wind calms, I can hear it ticking against my thigh. But mostly, I am watchless; it is a freedom. Now, instead of hours, I have mornings and afternoons, evenings and nights. My day is longer for it.

Chatting with the jewelry store owner as my battery was being installed, I looked down through the glass case and saw — Rolexes! This was new.

"Wow," I said. The owner was pleased I had noticed.

"Just got the dealership this week," he said. "Aren't they beautiful? A man of your stature should wear a Rolex."

Evidently, word of my oath of poverty had yet to reach him.

But like I said, town is good practice. I had my eye on the big gold one in the center of the display. The tag read $15,900.

"You know, it takes a year to make this watch," he said, taking it out of the case. "You could look at it as an investment."

"A man of my stature barely needs a calendar," I said.

"Eighteen karat gold," he said.

"I won't buy it," I said. "But I will try it on." He grinned and took it out of its case. Only in a small town.

"The ultimate status symbol," he said. "As a new dealer, I can work a one-time-only great deal."

Oh, he is relentless.

"You'll get comments everywhere you go," he said.

Yeah, I thought, like, "Your watch or your life."

I closed the clasp. Gold is warm against the skin, never cold like steel. A precision instrument, a work of art, it has a weight, a heft like ripe fruit. Suddenly my clothes looked shabby, my skin looked pasty, my truck, outside against the curb, looked under-equipped and over-oxidized.

I thanked him for the experience and took it off. Maybe I'd get a column out of it, I said.

He smiled and said be sure and mention that Rolexes are now available at his store in town. And now I have.

I drove home, put my town clothes in the closet, my watch on the dresser, and the seed in the feeder. Then I went to the woods.

I sat on the cabin porch and watched the leaves opening.

I didn't have a watch, but I knew when it was time to head back. It got dark.

Maypoles

The Rev. Billy Graham upsets us, or rather, his soundbite does.

Maybe you saw him, too, on the news from the White House, gold medal around his neck, warning of oblivion.

"We have confused liberty with license," he said. "As a nation, we are on the brink of self-destruction."

Warnings of Armageddon are nothing new. Self-proclaimed soothsayers have been shouting from the rooftops throughout history, "The end is near!" But we hear Billy Graham, and we feel some truth in it.

This comes at a bad time for us, pressed as we are to meet deadlines and confused by the evidences of chaos that seem to be gathering around us. Certainly, our own end is nearer.

Confused by what has passed, we worry about what is to come. Comfort, it seems, exists only in the moment. The moment is what we miss.

I am a country boy, and it is Spring; I find myself thinking of Maypoles. Outside, the day is filled with wind and crows. Flat-bottomed clouds stream over the woods. Under a riverine sky, it is as if we look downstream, inverted.

As a boy I would stand on a bridge over the creek that flowed through town and lean on the weathered concrete until the gravel left marks on my arms, stand and stare, unfocusing, until it was not the water that moved, but the bridge and me with it. Stand still on this hilltop. Watch the clouds pour over us. We flow.

This is the red maple's time to reign, their red crowns we see as hazy crescents among the treetops.

Beside a colony of opening Maypoles we sit, their canopies shining in the sun, the newest leaves still wrapped around their stems like parasols. The hard bud that first pushed through the loam swells now under their umbrellas. A waxy white flower will open, perhaps tomorrow, and the bees and the moths will come, the fruit will swell and yellow and sweeten.

May apples are edible. The pulp around the seeds can be made into jelly or eaten raw, and the juice makes a tasty lemonade.

Do not eat the plant itself; the stem and the leaf and the root are poisonous. Though used by native Americans and early settlers as a strong emetic and worm expellant, we dare not risk it. Besides, that coiling we felt in our gut was not from worms, but from living.

The wind cools and reaches under our jackets. There is rain in it. Violets in three colors shiver and gnats spin; treetops circle and shadows swim on our shoetops. The motion of the natural world stills what moves in us.

Here among Maypoles, under the sway of trees and the sliding sky, we find the old assurances.

Kinder Time

The girl calls from the city. She sounds vulnerable, maybe even frightened. A parent always worries.

"I'm fine, Dad, I guess," she says. "I woke up this morning and thought, 'What a beautiful day!' The cat was curled in the sunshine on the windowsill, and I could hear the birds singing above the traffic.

"I put the coffee on and stepped outside to get the paper. And there she was on the front page. My friend, Jeanette, on the front page. Her boyfriend had stabbed her to death."

The distance between the city and these mountains sometimes seems very great.

Jeanette worked in the children's bookstore across the street and would come over for coffee. She talked a lot about men. She was lonely.

In a world where sanity and stability seem qualities increasingly rare, loneliness, it turns out, can be a blessing.

"Then she told me about this big date. She was very excited. The guy was from downtown and was taking masseur classes. She introduced me to him at The Cafe, and it was weird how he'd sit there and stare at her.

"She was always asking me what I thought. I wasn't sure about him, and neither was she. But she was really lonely.

"I wrote a note to her parents though I've never met them. The world can be cruel, I said, but I hoped that time would be kinder to them."

Kinder time. May we all know kinder time.

She feels better now, she says, and by that same degree do I feel worse. This is a parent's function.

We say our I-love-yous. I go outside in search of reassurance. I spread a blanket in the field.

Sunlight rolls warm up the slope and covers me. Blue-bellied clouds stream out of the west, casting their shadows over the hills. I hear the wind effervescent in the tender leaves, watch it flow through the boughs of the treeline. I smell lilacs.

Robins hop through the gleaming grass, bees search for clover, jays call. Finches circle above the house. The dog sleeps in the shade of the stable. Bullfrogs garump in the pond. A beetle inspects my knee. I find comfort in such things. These are things we can count on. This is what we seek.

Feeling the need to get away, to regain our confidence in the goodness of life, we would travel a thousand miles for this. Peace is closer than we think.

I stretch out in the field, here where time is kind. I remember the ache of youth. I wish she was here.

Veggie Dreams

Ignoring the oaks, I planted my garden this morning. I will be replanting soon, I think.

The oaks, according to local belief, signal when it's time to put in your corn. It's time, country people say, when the oak leaves are as big as a mouse's ear.

Well, I just walked across the wet field to check, and the oak leaves are still in a tight wrap. If these were mice, they'd be as deaf as acorns.

It is also worth noting that to walk comfortably across the field I wore my lined field jacket, the same one I wear to the woods all winter. Halfway across, I put on my gloves.

Back at the house, I filled the log bin. Smoke curls out of the chimney. This is the end of May. In these mountains, we could be just 100 days away from our first frost, having not yet seen our last.

Wendell Berry's grandmother used to tell him that the day is coming when we will not know the summer from the winter but by the budding of the trees.

Berry is a writer I admire. He worked his grandfather's hillside farm in Kentucky with mules. He believes that small farms and small towns could be the salvation of this nation. I believe Wendell Berry. And, this spring especially, I believe his grandma, too.

My garden holds an elevated significance this year. This year I'm hoping it will feed me.

You can live off of your garden. It is possible. I know a guy who did it. For a full year he lived off of the production of a small patch of forked yard in front of his apartment. In New Jersey. He says he even had enough to give away to friends. (Scatter! Here comes Euell with another bag of zucchini!)

His friends, I'm sure, still like him the same even after malnutrition ruined his teeth. Looks aren't everything. So what if he'll never be on the cover of Organic Gardening, he survived.

So my corn may be doomed to rot in the ground, the earth being too cold. But I'm not worried about the zucchini.

Zucchini, I am convinced, are the Schwarzeneggers of the vegetable world. I could've planted them on Groundhog Day and still had enough green clubs to sell to summer tourists at outlet prices.

Now there's an idea. I'm on the lookout for ideas of late, especially ones that will produce income without poisoning my Muse, even if she is no more vigorous than someone who has lived for an entire year on yard greens.

Yeah. I could plow the field and sow zucchini, then squander three months writing and golfing. Come September, I'll borrow the township dump truck and haul the gonzo gourds out to the road. I'll build a plywood shack and handpaint a sign that proclaims, "Support the Arts. Eat Zukes!"

Too esoteric, you say? Could be. But it beats, "Will Write for Food," which was my original idea.

But I know zucchini. It's not like I can corner the market. Well-meaning lovers of the humanities will stop and donate to my cause sackfuls of their own.

Too bad zucchinis won't ferment. Corn will, of course, and what a fine, old mountain tradition that is. With this year's crop, though, I don't figure I could distill enough moonshine to raise even a frown from the Methodist Church Women. Things are tough all over.

I've got it. Mark your calendars for the First Annual Upper Turkeyfoot Zucchini Festival!

Miss Zucchini will be crowned! Zucchini Pitching! Zucchini Crafts! Zucchini Carving Demonstrations! Zucchini Bake-Off! Zucchini Demolition Derby! Zucchini Donkey Basketball! Greased Zucchini Contest! Zucchini Opera (Puccini Zucchini)!

I know genius when I feel it. Quick, somebody call Burpee.

I need a sponsor.

Sons

Near the end of the viewing, during a rare break in the line of mourners, my brother sat down between his wife and daughter who still stood benumbed and looking toward the doorway, and he aged before my eyes.

He sat with his elbows on his knees and his fists together, desperately stoic, his face flushed with grief, and he looked at the pictures of his son pinned to the cork board beside the closed casket.

It haunted me as I flew home. My own son pulled into my driveway as I lifted the bags from the trunk. He hugged me, and I held onto him a little longer than I usually do.

For years I have kept a journal. Most of them have vanished, but I found this today. It is a comfort. Indulge me.

Cruelty and love exist in this world. We have some say in the balance. Here, then, is a moment from an age ago, a reminder of priorities:

* * *

Too dark to see the ball now, so we hang our gloves on the nails in the garage and head for the house. The grass really should have been cut, I'm thinking, when he reminds me.

"We've gotta get milk, Dad," he says. "Can I drive?"

He never misses a chance. Nine-year-olds are like that.

On the ball field he wants to pitch, he wants to catch, he wants to play second and center and short. In the workshop he wants to pound nails, cut wood, drill holes, repair chain saws, construct airplanes. In the office he wants to write a story on the typewriter, divide on the calculator, insult his sister on the computer.

He wants to do it all. Can I? He wants to be like me. Can I? Can I?

"Sure," I say. "You can drive."

He runs into the house for the cans. He emerges with a wax paper tube of Ritz crackers. He has to go back for the cans.

Into the pickup we climb. I sit against the door and work the clutch. He does the rest, peering through the steering wheel. His muscles work warm against my side. At the corner of his mouth, his tongue makes an ocassional appearance.

This is illegal, I know. But the road is straight and open and dirt. Besides, driving makes him concentrate. It's one of the rare times he ceases emitting engine noises, controlling, instead, the real thing.

As an instructor, I am patient. I issue one word commands. I am ruining my digestion.

"Gas," I say. "Second. Good. Brake. Easy."

"I'll try not to hit that bird," he says, swerving. I see no bird.

"Smooth," I say. "Everything smooth."

He stomps on the brake. My head snaps forward.

"What was that?" I say.

"Dead 'possum," he says. "Can't run over the dead 'possum." His respect heartens me.

We coast to an even stop in front of the milkhouse. I award him a Ritz. He disappears into the barn to say hello to the cows while I dip milk from the bulk tank. On the way back, his skills desert him. Third-to-second proves confusing, and he hits reverse. The gnashing of metal stabs at my gut.

"Sorry, Dad," he says, basset eyed. His remorse is short-lived. Close to home now, and despite my objections he keeps swiveling 180 degrees to look out the back window and admire his dust.

"Road," I say. "Road. Road. Road."

Elsewhere on this planet, men are making history, creating beauty, seeking truth.

Me, I'm with my boy in the ditch.

It is enough.

Commencing at 77

My mother graduated from college this spring. Cum Laude. It took her 60 years. I think she is a hero.

In the fall of 1937 she sat in her first class at Westminster College. Between then and now came The War and marriage and children and job and family and promotions and retirement, and all the despair and rapture of living.

Now, there she stood among the graduates lined up in their caps and gowns, one petite, silver-curled lady among them, flushed and beaming in the sun, and they waited.

Mom thinks they were waiting for the Governor, not that she minded. She holds public servants in high esteem, especially when they are Republicans and winners of the Silver Star.

But the sun was strong, and the gowns were hot, and she was glad when the helicopter passed low over Old Main, sure that the Governor had just arrived.

Most of us were there, seated under the leafing maples on folding oak chairs with a funeral home stenciled on the backs: Cousin Dale, who left behind his congregation in Seattle; Brother Jay, who left behind his insurance office in New England; Cousin Jill, who left behind her body-parts-art collection on Waugh Avenue (this is, after all, a college town) just a few blocks away.

Aunt Aileen, a proud member of the American Civil Liberties Union and a subscriber to avante-garde publications, had walked over from Vine Street.

Even Aunt Margie, a retired Army nurse full of tales, rode in from Indianapolis with Uncle Gordon. Uncle Gordon is determined to single-handedly rid Western Pennsylvania of groundhogs, and his presence at commencement honored us all, even though he didn't stay until the end.

Step-sisters Susan (from Atlanta) and Pat were there, too. Their father and my mother married late in life. They had attended the same one-room school. He tried to live long enough to see this day, accepting, for a while, treatment I think he would have otherwise refused.

Being 77 and a student, Mom had gained a bit of local fame — you know, the never-too-late angle.

"I don't know what all the damn fuss is about," he would bluster, but you could tell he was as proud of her as anybody.

"I just hope she finds a job when she graduates," was his standard line. He died this spring, but he was there, too, because he said he would be.

Seattle, Atlanta, Philadelphia, Maine, Indianapolis, New Wilmington, Upper Turkeyfoot, all seated in the dappled light straining for a glimpse of her as the procession began.

She was easy to find, really. Mom, who will tell you she used to be five feet tall, walked the begonia-lined quad immediately in front of a young man of six-foot-ten. Her pace was brisk, there was no gap in the line. Once she even left the big guy behind; he had turned to wave and had to catch up with one great stride.

They sat then in the sun, ivy-covered walls a background for the higher-educated, and listened to the Governor.

The Governor said we wouldn't remember anything he said. He was right. But he also said we would remember only that it was short. Sometimes even Silver Medal winners can be wrong.

The speeches and the reading of the names and the awarding of diplomas took hours. They sat in the searing sun, in black robes, this their final test.

I took a picture with a long lens as the Governor shook her hand. We all cheered. She may have wanted to say something to him about the gas tax, but this was not the time. She could always write him later, which she just might do, after she spruces up her resume.

Son Weds

Under the trees they drove and into the shaded hollow, balloons quaking and ribbons streaming, "Just Married" on the trunk.

I watched them go, my son and his bride, and something in me moved ahead. Something which I cannot name went with them down the mountainside and left me in the church parking lot.

The wedding was wonderful. All went as planned.

The minister's words were relevant and wise. The music was pure and moving. The wedding party attended to their duties with poise and compassion.

Even the two-year-old flower girl walked the aisle as if she were royalty, unlike rehearsal the evening before when her brother dragged her by the arm as she lay squalling on the carpet.

And my son. My son. Broad-shouldered, sweating a little, loving a lot, oblivious to everything else once the center of his life appeared at the back of the church.

You know how it goes. Her father joined their hands. The mothers wiped their tears. Candles lit. Rings exchanged. Vows made.

"You may never be happier than you are at this moment," the minister said. "This may be as good as it gets," he said. Commitment, for better, for worse.

The young man's mother and I sat in the first pew, the necessary distance between us. Divorced eight years, we had exchanged one brief glance when first she took her seat, then looked away, the velocity of memory more than we could bear.

The new Mr. and Mrs. O'Brien were presented to applause. We followed them into the sunshine and formed a receiving line. A couple of my ex-in-laws even shook my hand. Some people I didn't know embraced my son's mother then turned their backs.

It didn't bother me then for life is short, and I was full of joy. My son and my daughter-in-law are young and sensible and hard-working. They share a bond unique to those whose childhood friendship bloomed.

We stood upwind and blew bubbles, the wind doing most of the work, all of us children again for a moment.

We walked down the steep path to the fellowship hall festooned with silver and blue and rich with the smells of home cooking. No caterers needed here. Family and neighbors and members of the congregation pitch in. Country people pride themselves on self-reliance. Why, the father of the bride, I'm told, made the baked beans, stirring in pieces of bacon he had cured himself.

We found our seats, name cards for the families of the bride and groom thoughtfully arranged, my daughter's boyfriend serving as a sort of buffer zone, poor guy.

But this was my son's day, and his wife's. Her family is kind and strong, as is their faith. I could not be more pleased.

They prepared to leave at last, after the table-rapping and the whooping and the cutting of the cake, after the picture-taking and the punch-toasting, and the thanking. They said their farewells and headed for their car.

I climbed the hill to the church parking lot. I found myself alone, surrounded by moments from his childhood.

I heard the doctor on the waiting room phone say, "You have a son." I felt him stiffen against my chest in the middle of the night, colicky and refusing the bottle. I heard his head hit the tub when he took his first shower and got so excited he jumped up and down. I saw him lying in traction after he leaped from the logshed roof, bravely facing his first night alone in the hospital. I felt him warm against me as he stood on the seat between my knees and steered the truck down the dirt road, swerving to miss what he claimed was a dead 'possum, looking over his shoulder to admire the dust in our wake. I watched him stretch to reach that first high step of the bus on his first day of school, then wipe a circle in the steamed-up window to wave. I watched him hit homeruns and throw strikes and tell jokes and notice girls and … and I marveled at how much I had missed.

Up the hill they came and stopped. We shared a moment on the hilltop as they began their life together. It was a gift. Then down the road they drove and under the trees.

They will be fine. They will be fine.

In a Field Unmowed

No one can see me.

Tall grasses surround me. Sky covers me. I lie on the hillside, hidden deep in the unmowed field.

To some, this field may look unkempt. To some, this field may seem unused, uncultivated, wasted. But I use it.

I use it to walk in and scare up the grasshoppers. I use it to see the face of the wind. I use it to strengthen my grip on the earth, on the moment. I use it, and I let it be.

Events dominate life, if we let them. Weddings and funerals, celebrations and wakes, adventures and consequences. An afternoon such as this, free from appointments, fate at arm's length, is a blessing.

I flip off my moccasins, pull my workshirt over my head, and stretch out to watch the clouds pass.

Do I bore you? Would you rather read of tragedy and triumph? Ah, patience, my friend. Those shall find you. None of us escapes.

Let it be enough, for now, to watch the gray-bellied cumulus drift under high stratus. Drifting, let it be enough. Let it be enough to be. (Go ahead. Hum the Beatles song if you like.)

"May you lead an eventful life" is a Chinese curse. I understand it.

"Keep your affairs as but one or two," Thoreau wrote, "and keep your accounts on your thumbnail."

What a simple, peaceful way to live, yet how difficult to achieve.

I have spoken here before of the pure present, of that moment which Theodore Roethke describes as when "the small drop forms, but does not fall."

This can be such a moment. It is up to us.

Lie here in the green and blooming field, if only for an hour, turning with the earth, spinning with the planets, hurtling through the endless void — oh, it is too much to grasp, but what a gift it is to take the time, to pause long enough to consider the big questions.

I have noticed lately how often the cat looks at the world upside down. I try that now, and am amused. I put my forehead in the lacy beginnings of Queen Anne's lace, and am moved by the beauty of the tall grasses against the sky. It is a fresh view. To appreciate the ordinary, we have only to turn it upside down. This is why reflections on a pond please us so.

We discover in them a frog's perspective, otherwise unavailable unless we were to lie in the rushes submerged to our nostrils.

The spit bugs have been busy on the fleabane and the clover, the tender nymphs content in their bubbles. Far off, I see the tossing blue ridges of the Alleghenies, closer, the shimmering crowns of trees in full leaf, wind moving through them with the sound of surf, grasses bowing. A small brown ant crawls down the bearded plantain and bites me on the arm.

This is a world that takes care of itself, self-contained and overflowing, where distance always gathers back to nearness.

I can only begin to tell you of the sheen on each leaf, of the iridescent daisies and the tiny insects on their centers like pepper on yolk, of the sparrows settling into the rivers of wind that flow through the field.

I can only list the blue spires of basil in bloom, the yellow varnish of cinquefoil, the hoverfly that stares me in the eye, the red-tailed hawks that turn on the thermals of the afternoon, so high I would have never seen them had I not been on my back staring at the sky.

The interval, the pause between events, can sustain us if we let it.

Summer

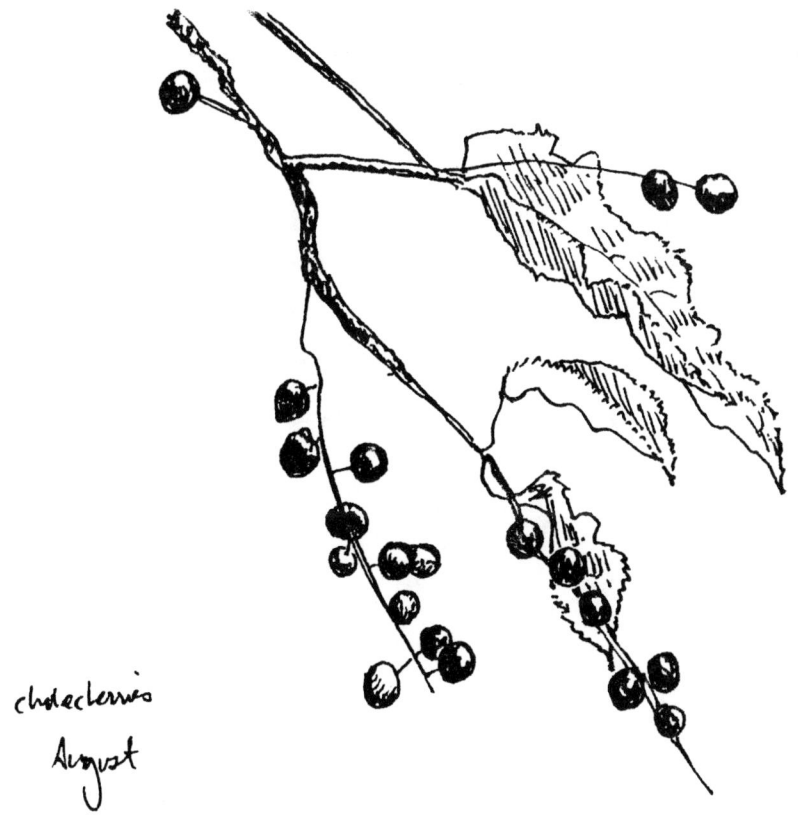

chokecherries
August

Impulse Toward Ripeness

The field matures.

I have telephoned the farmer who makes the hay that grows there. His wife answered in the milking parlor. Milking machines clicked and slurped in the background.

"If you don't need the hay," I said, "I think I'll let the field grow up."

The field is my own, yet I feel a certain guilt. I hope they will not miss the two or three wagonloads of timothy now chest high and bowing in the wind.

Their Holstein, I know, produce best on a richer crop of clover and alfalfa. The farmer and his sons, I think, mow the field more as a favor to me than because they really need the hay.

I hope I am right about that. If I am wrong, they will not tell me. They are good neighbors.

To me, a field going back to woods is a thing of beauty.

Already (just three years has the field lain fallow) this spring there bloomed daisy fleabane, sheep sorrel, cinquefoil, evening lychnis, purple and white musk mallow, red clover, oxeye daisies and wild basil. Already I find Queen Anne's lace sprouting and wild sunflowers budding.

I await the spread of asters and goldenrod. I am anxious for blackberries to arch over rabbit warrens. I want to see tiger moth caterpillars on milkweed and goldfinches on thistle. I want to hear the owls at dusk as they come to hunt the mice that tunnel in the grass.

I want to watch the trees return — first the locusts and the ashes, then the red maples and the black birches, then the cherries and the sugars and the oaks.

So, the field matures. Grasses go to seed. The things that live there proceed toward their natural end — but there shall be more beginnings than endings.

Fullness of life, as Logan Pearsall Smith said, is the goal of everything that lives: the impulse toward completeness, toward ripeness and self-realization, is the most compelling of all motives.

This Pennsylvania landscape is forest by nature. The forces that compel these hills to woodland are already at work. I feel it, sitting in the field this evening, I feel the rush to ripeness.

I feel it in the bearded timothy swaying against the racing indigo clouds.

I feel it in the songs of birds echoing from their roosts deep in the dark wood.

I feel it in the crescent blade of the new moon shining in the salmon sky.

I feel it in the cricket chortling beside me.

I feel it in the moth that stutters through the blades. I feel it in the ant that crawls across my thigh and climbs onto the page.

The wind rises cool against my shins, and there I feel it, too.

I feel it in the spires of pines and in horizons tossing black against the sky, and in the neon course of fireflies.

I feel it in the vapor and the dusk.

This impulse toward completion I feel within myself, sitting in this field at sunset, this night rising around me, this world ripening at the end of June. I shall watch the field return to woods. I look forward to the show.

Farm Vanishing

There's a farm nearby that stands abandoned. I pass it sometimes when I go out the back way and take the shortcut to the Ridge Road. It makes me sad.

The farmer is dead. His pickup truck sits rusting in the pasture with the hood open and weeds growing up through the engine compartment. Paint flakes off the barn.

It is a small farm, just big enough for a few Holsteins. But the man who made it work was proud of this place. You could tell.

Driving through his farm would lift my spirits. The road bends between the house and the equipment shed, and the grass was always cropped right up to the edge of the macadam. He would show me the broad flat of his hand and his smile when I passed.

I liked seeing the white ducks waggling their tails on the dark pond below the road. Some of the biggest hydrangeas I know of drooped huge and blue around his porch.

Cliff was no gentleman farmer. From these hundred acres he extracted a living, such as it was. He wasn't in it for the money. No shiny new club cab in the driveway. No air-conditioned, dual-wheeled juggernaut in the fields. Cliff made do with the same pickup year after year, and with the same old Farmall, its tire treads nearly gone.

No, financial gain was not the reason Cliff farmed. I'd say it was the way of life that appealed to him.

This probably sounds sentimental to my neighbors working bigger farms, exhausted as they are this time of year with the planting finally finished, worried about too much rain to mow hay and not enough to grow corn, and the milking to do, always the milking to do.

But Cliff's was a smaller view, a slower pace. Even when his hip got so bad that crossing the road became an adventure, even when I'd have to slow down to give him time, even then he'd wave and grin. He seemed perpetually close to laughter as if the joke were on him, and wasn't life a real knee-slapper after all?

I like to think that Cliff believed that less is more, and that his mortality came as no surprise to him.

The farm stands abandoned because no son succeeds him. There exists no young man (or courageous young woman) to take over, no one who believes he will be forever strong and fit and who loves the land enough to be imprisoned by it, no sinewy youth brimming with faith and confidence and willing to assume the cycle of planting and borrowing.

So weeds grow up through the engine compartment, and muskrats invade the pond. Paint flakes off the barn, and the pickup sits in the overgrown pasture with its hood up as if its spirit had escaped like the mist that rises from the blue valley.

Oh, there remain a few signs of activity. Beef steers stand stupified in a muddy feed lot. Someone has pulled into the yard and left tracks in the grass gone to seed.

The farm will be soon sold, I imagine. Perhaps the heirs are fighting over their percentage. It happens so often. And the land will be subdivided. Summer homes already surround the fields.

What Cliff had worked so hard for didn't last long. In fact, it barely outlasted him, groundhogs moving into the cellar, ash trees sprouting in the fields, the land closing up in his wake.

So, too, will those things for which we strive evaporate. Nothing lasts. Let us remind ourselves every day.

The joys of living, it seems, rest not in what we think are major accomplishments, not in success nor fame nor wealth, but in the smaller things, in a gleam of a feather floating on the pond, in the musk of walnuts dropping in the yard, in June bugs banging their heads against the screen.

While he farmed, Cliff enjoyed the work. Dying, as Red Smith said, is no big deal. The least of us will accomplish that. Living is the trick.

Mountain Golf

Passion has entered my life. I've taken up golf.

I play mostly on a course on the other side of the mountain.

It is no country club.

Private courses have their unreasonable expectations: no jeans, no T-shirts, no coolers full of beer strapped to the backs of the carts. But on league night on my home course, an ice chest is the main reason to ride.

The guys can't wait for league night. You can tell by the way they wheel into the parking lot with the gravel flying. From their pickups they spring, slinging their bags over their shoulders and popping their tops.

For a couple of hours once a week they have no job, no mortgage, no wife demanding new aluminum siding. They're standing on the greensward in the open air under the blue sky. Life is good. It is, at least, until they hook the first tee shot into the woods.

I have heard golf called a gentleman's game. Most of the guys I play with would take offense to being called gentle. They only do that to psyche each other when arm wrestling. This, after all, is mountain golf. But they are honorable.

So maybe they wear cutoffs and tank tops. Maybe their lower lips bulge with snuff. Maybe they'll pull from their canvas bag a wood they bought in 1982 at Giant Eagle for four bucks and take a whack at a ball marked with Xs.

No, mountain golf is not for poseurs.

But these are honorable men. Why, I've heard about a guy that was drummed out of the league for cheating. This, you must realize, is the sport where Bobby Jones once gave up a national championship by penalizing himself a stroke. When lauded for his honesty, he said, "You might as well praise a man for not robbing a bank."

Famously difficult, golf is good for the soul. Temptations abound — the temptation to move your ball away from the tree trunk, the temptation to whiff and pretend it was a practice swing, the temptation to brag you broke 100.

The game is a form of moral effort. As one social observer put it, a golf course is the best place to watch ministers.

This game tests your character. Maybe you hit a beauty over the trees and land it in front of the green. You walk to the ball accepting the applause of your fellows, and you take a wedge, and you launch a divot the size of a trout, and there sits the ball, mocking you. Such humiliations are the essence of golf.

Like the other day. In the heat of the evening I bent over a short putt. Sweat ran out from under my cap and splashed on my clubhead. The sun uncovered and long shadows crossed my path. Butterflies were making an uproar in the field. A biting fly drank from the back of my neck. I never had a chance.

My opponent patted me on the back.

"I know how it feels," he said. "But that was one helluva second shot to even get there!"

Praise for what is done well, and sympathy for what isn't.

Life should be like that.

The Sanity of Summer

Let us step back for a few minutes from the rampage of the stock market, from the President's hormones, and from the alarming reports of Chinese military-capitalists selling AK47s to American street gangs.

Let us pause to acknowledge the season. In a world gone mad, we find sanity in summer.

Overnight, it seems, the pasture grasses rise high enough to hide in; redtop and fescue and timothy grace the hilltop, tall enough to be flattened by rain, leaving circles where the fairies romped (I'm Irish, don't forget), where a man can sit enveloped in green under the deep sky.

Off the roof rain runs in braids that, depending on the wind, slap against flat stones or rumble in the watering can whose galvanized spout empties into a second can whose spout empties into the flower bed.

From the end of his gutter, a friend has hooked a chain for the rain to follow, ringing the small brass bells he tied there, rain chimes. He saw it in Japan, he says. Respected and revered, the rain in Japanese is kamisama, a spirit, alive.

Deer flies, striped-wing devils, torment us in the sun. A robin complains of our presence. Eggshells lie under its nest in the eaves of the coop, a second brood hatched. The garter snake that has lived there for five years has shed its skin in the grass, bursting out head first, the vacated tail hooked into the earth.

Big events, these, if we are so blessed.

At mid-day what we notice most is silence. The cicadas are soon to fill the void, but for now, the raucous trill of spring has ceased with the heat. Birds gasp deep in the glen. Bullfrogs soak in the reeds.

Yet for all of this, the hour after sunset holds the magic. Before the moon rises out of the woods, the field ripples with the light of fireflies. If you let your eyes unfocus and take it all in, the broad field undulates like the swells of the sea.

Lightning bugs flash to attract mates. Everyone knows that. Other insects produce light, but only fireflies flash, only fireflies signal.

The larvae overwinter in underground cells, pupate in hot weather and and emerge as adults, mate, lay their eggs on the surface or just under the soil. Hatching in a month, the larvae feed on snails and slugs and other soft-bodied insects, including, yes, fireflies.

Little else is known. As is so often the case, what is closest to us is least understood. The true mysteries lie in the visible, not the invisible.

Whether the adults feed at all is debated. The males do all the flying while the females, some even wingless, crawl about or sit placidly flashing their desire.

At least three species of fireflies inhabit my field. I note the different flashes, some long and yellow, emitted while rising so it forms a "J" with great distances flown in between, some in rapid greenish pulses of three flashes each marked by fast and erratic flight.

On the ground or clinging to weedstalks, some females can be a regular as beacons. You, too, can call in the males with a small flashlight, turned on for one second at two-second intervals. The kids will love it.

The females answer only the males of their own species, mate, and stop flashing. At least one naturalist is convinced that some females mate, then signal only to males of other species, hoping for a meal.

I leave the similes to you.

You see? You can still smile. Real wonders exist just outside your door. Turn off the air conditioner and the computer and the television and the lights. Sit outside in the the dark with those you love. Watch the fireflies and the moonrise. Feel the permanence of cycles.

Best Action is No Action

The university calls experts to the capital. I got a pamphlet in my mailbox. They will convene on conserving natural diversity. Count me out.

Their work is important. But I'm not going.

Firstly, because I am no expert. Secondly, because in a room full of academics and administrators there is sure to be talk of "facilitating outcomes," and such language makes my head tight.

I am for natural diversity, as my neighbors can tell you. My field is returning to woods by degrees. I leave it alone. It pleases me to watch the species returning, although I'm guessing that where I see small miracles, a neighbor or two may see only weeds and vermin.

I sit in the middle of the field now, rapping away on this heavy, old, wonderful Smith-Corona with the grasses swaying around me. In the west, the sky darkens to indigo. In the southwest, mist obscures the five ridges beneath the darkness of a gathering storm.

It will rain on me, I think.

Thunder pounds its kettledrums in the south, and by looking straight up at the last shreds of blue, I see by the drift that the storm is headed this way. The dogs lie against my ankles; they sniff the rising wind. I wait.

I have set up this portable chair and this rusting, collapsible (at any moment) snack tray among the opening daisies and cinquefoil. I have carried the old typewriter on my shoulder and ignored the cramp. I will sit for a while yet.

Burgeoning diversity surrounds me. The green tribes show themselves.

Settlements of goldenrod, half grown, rise above the grasses. Canada goldenrod it is, clones, you know, reproducing from spreading roots called rhizomes. The plants are genetically identical, yet each distinctly itself, formed by its unique afflictions and batterings, which, of course, makes us who we are as well.

Milkweed, too, colonizes the ground, promising us tiger moths and monarchs and a thousand miracles of chrysalis if we seek them out. Asters rise a paler green, and blackberries bloom in arches, thickets of pleasure and pain.

The thunder increases. The first cold drops splash on my arms and legs, which I slap from time to time, the deer flies having found me, thorns of summer. But there is time. The cardinals still sing, the barn swallows streak low over the field, and a tree swallow darts past — still time to feed before the rain intensifies. I wait.

I see the spread of wild sunflowers, still a month from flowering. Their increase pleases me, as do the sparrows and the blackbirds settling back into green after my approach. It doesn't take long. A few minutes. They don't seem to mind the clacking of the keys.

Even the grasses themselves, when you look, stand in families — the redtop and the timothy, the bluegrass and the bottlebrush and the meadow grass in tall, tropical clumps.

I know, too, that the creatures have multiplied — the voles and the mice and the rabbits. I know it by the kestrel that hovers each day above the hilltop, flapping and stationary, and by the red-tailed hawks higher up in their widening gyre, and by the owl that glides through the dusk, as silent and efficient as a blade.

The page goes limp in the carriage. The hissing in wooded valley tells me it's time to move. I set up in the stable with the doors open and finish this as the rain marches through the leaves. We were speaking of diversity.

I read the pamphlet. It tells of "facilitated small groups discuss(ing) conceptual framework and cooperative action agenda." My head tightens.

Their goal is to "develop regional sustainable development approaches." Though laudable on the surface, I am worried. I see in this the vanity of men, that high opinion of ourselves which causes us to meddle. Ego leads to action, when all we have to do is nothing. Do nothing (which implies, of course, neither harming nor helping), and diversity happens in its own sweet time. I see the proof before me.

In the field untouched, the web of life thickens. It includes me, too.

Today's methods will in the future be considered as crude and as ignorant as those of the past. Why should we believe we have answers, when we do not even understand something as ordinary as why a liquid is a liquid?

So while in Harrisburg this fall experts and administrators will facilitate and framework, I hope to be sitting in this field watching life diversify without my help, letting it be.

Home for the Summer

Shorty sits on his porch and watches the wind in the trees.

Aileen, his wife of more than 50 years, asks from the swing if anybody wants anything. Nobody does. They have come to be with Shorty before he dies.

A neighbor stops on the sidewalk and says hello over the strawberry bush. "How you doing, Shorty?" he says. In a small town, everybody knows.

"Oh, I'm a-doin', Hilton," Shorty says. It has been nearly a month since the doctors removed most of his stomach and pancreas.

"Taking any treatment?" Hilton asks.

"No," Shorty says. "They've stopped all that. How's the electric?"

Shorty and Hilton are both retired from the college, Hilton as professor of Greek and Roman classics, Shorty as electrician.

"Not so good," Hilton says "But I can live with it." Leaves rustle in the wind. "I hope you can, too."

The conversation tires Shorty. He rises with difficulty but without assistance and makes his way unsteadily to the bed set up in the living room. This is a recent change. Just last week he would sit and talk for as long as there was company.

He'd talk about his father and his youth. He'd talk about the farm. Someone might mention that the timber was being cut on the old Saylor place, and Shorty would talk about logging.

"I hated that," he'd laugh. "That chain dragging in the snow and your gloves wet. Most of those old horses were hard in the mouth. They'd either stop short, or long, and you'd have to circle around one more time to hook up."

Shorty could always tell a good story. Often it was about how his older brothers forced him to learn the fiddle, and how they played first at Saturday night house dances, standing on the stairs while couples danced in the two front rooms with the rugs rolled up and the furniture carried out onto the porch, then at Grange halls and county fairs and then on the radio every morning at milking time.

Oh, maybe you had heard the stories before, but they still made you smile.

Shorty tires easily now. Through the window you can see Aileen cover him as he lies on his side. Her hand lingers on his hip.

She rejoins the family on the porch. They look into each others eyes, words unnecessary, accepting what they cannot change. Aileen is the only one to speak. She says, "Me, too."

Before he went inside, Shorty had said good-bye. "See you," he had said.

And he had said something else. An Amish buggy had passed, a young woman driving, wire-rimmed glasses and black bonnet, reins in her hands, the flush of summer on her cheeks, the horse's hooves clopping and the spoked wheels clattering over the brick street.

There on the porch with neighbors stopping by and the strawberry bush in bloom, there with wind in the trees and family around, Shorty had said something else.

"It's good to be home," he had said.

Everybody knew that to be true.

Reunion Alert

Another high school reunion approaches. I don't feel like telling you which one, but my wife will. She thinks it's funny.

There's an age difference thing at work here. We joke about it all the time. Except lately she seems to be doing most of the laughing.

Now, with all modesty, I can say that I am not yet wizened. But my wife, with her cheerful disposition and her favorite ballcap and T-shirt, can look like she should be thinking about the prom instead of my 35th reunion, which is one of the subjects she has been most cheerful about of late.

Her fun began just after I took a call from Don Badger. Don had exhibited organizational skills as president of the camera club, so it comes as no surprise that he should be leading the conspiracy to assemble the Class of '63 that we might assess the degree of each other's ruin.

That's what I thought as I heard myself saying, sure July would work for me.

"Thirty-five," I said after I hung up, disoriented. I mean, here we are, living our lives, goals still ahead of us, striving to create truth and beauty and deluded enough to think we're just getting started and — and Don Badger calls, rips us out of the present and catapults us into the past. Jumping off a train must be like that.

"Oh, you have to go," said my wife of the pleasing personality as she ripped out a page from the magazine she had been reading and handed it to me.

"Here," she beamed. "You'll want this." It was a moisturizer sample.

"I don't need moisture," I said.

"Oh, but, 'It's more than just a moisturizer,'" she said, tapping the page.

Seems it has pure vitamin E delivered to the skin by patented microspheres.

"'Skin looks smoother in just one day,'" she read on. "'Healthier in just two weeks.'" Oh, she was enjoying herself.

"You could start today," she said, "and by the reunion you could look like you're 10!"

She made me laugh. Then I stepped outside to do pushups on the porch. I can do more than 35.

I make plans. If the swelling in my knee recedes, I can maybe jog a few miles before July. I'll want to be tan and toned when I walk into the Knights of Columbus Hall. So, okay, smooth would be good, too.

I wait until she's entranced by "Party of Five," and sneak a look at her magazine. I scan Glamour's 103 Best Beauty Tricks, which doesn't take as long as you might think, half of them having to do with hair, from which I am freed. This, of course, makes the skin that much more significant.

I go to the bathroom mirror and take a hard look at myself. Sure, a few lines and creases, but, all in all, not too bad, as long as I remember to keep my chin up, which is always good advice.

Still, a "finished yet dewy look" would be nice. It says after applying moisturizer to your whole face, powder your T-zone only. It says your cheeks are the only place you want to look dewy.

I'm not sure what my T-zone is, but this is "Glamour" and not "Cosmo," so I'm guessing it's my forehead, nose, and chin. In my case, however, it's more of an M-zone. I'll bet this is where patented microspheres are invaluable.

In any event, I decide I don't want to be dewy anyplace. That will happen of its own accord, what with all the stress.

Actually, I don't think I want to go. Ten years ago I went, and I still haven't recovered. A startling vision comes back to me — a group of glassy-eyed, middle-aged goofs forming a circle and doing the chicken dance.

The highlight of the evening was when Don Badger showed slides of graduation, and of every reunion since. It was like watching death advance in five-year increments. It would have been completely sobering if it weren't for one of my old buds whooping and pointing out former spouses.

Still, it might be fun. Especially if I can rescue myself from the brink of geezerdom. I rip open the sample. Tell my wife at your peril.

The Old Home Place

Through thigh-deep skunk cabbage I stepped, careful not to break a leaf; the rich, black earth of the floodplain clumped on my loafers. Using the roots of an old maple as steps, I climbed the bank and slipped down the other side to stand among wild phlox in bloom and watch the water slip over the stones. What I saw next made my heart leap.

How I came to be here is not easy to explain. It's just that the big road has been finished now for a few years, and I found myself at the other end of it, less than an hour away from this bend in the creek, and when I passed under the huge green signs that directed me north or south, I took the long way home.

I drove until the highway ran out, then followed my instincts over narrow macadam, the center black with tar.

I was raised not far from here. Twenty miles. Yet it has always been these few bends in the creek that have felt most like home to me. There is something here I do not understand, a pull in the chest, a sense of peace. Flowing water will do that to me, or is it something more, something bred in the blood? Surely, such a place exists for you. I hope it does.

I meant to drive through this tiny village along the creek and be on my way. But I found myself pulling off the road and turning off the engine, and wading through the skunk cabbage to stand in phlox blooming at the water's edge.

I own a picture of my grandmother swimming here, she and her girlfriends in their long black sleeves and their hair up in ruffled caps. Yes, this would be about the spot, here where the creek widens and the sun hits the water, and the old iron bridge spans the rapids in the distance.

I wonder if any of those girls are still alive, and as I wonder, a great blue heron lifts out of the creek and with slow, powerful wing beats it rises above the treetops, water trailing from its feet in golden strands. It turns and flies straight over the house of my great-grandfather.

How easy to find meaning in such moments. How they quicken the heart.

In that house my grandfather wooed my grandmother. They took long walks on the railroad tracks that ran behind the house; I know because I have a picture of him with his arms around her, lifting her off the rails, her feet kicking the air, and a look of pure joy on both their faces. He wears his doughboy uniform. It was days before their marriage.

My mother was born in that house, in the front bedroom that opened to the orchard and the mill beyond. A few ravaged apple trees still mark the edge of the mill race reduced now to a marsh, and the mill to a foundation in the weeds. But the house stands, as does the towering oak in the front yard where that wizened old man used to sit and rock and watch the creek and curse Truman.

It was all I could do to stop myself from walking through the yard and knocking on the door and making whomever lives inside an offer. I would unseal the spring house and reopen the main fireplace. I would peel back the flooring to expose the trap door I know is there in the kitchen, and the cool dark of the root cellar below. I would sit under the oak and rock and watch the creek.

I think sometimes of going home. And would I dream then of these misted, tossing horizons, and of the sunset pink on the bellies of the clouds that stream over these mountains and me? Ah, the soul aches, but for what? Know that, and you have wisdom.

Sit

Stay a while.

The grass is cropped, the pickup washed, and the supper dishes are in the sink. Oh, yes, the garden needs tilling, but there is tomorrow.

Let us go now while we still have an hour of light. Listen to the crickets sing! Today, for the first time, it seems summer.

Best take a coat. The sun tingles in our skin, and the northeast breeze has a chill in it. Let us leave the house if only for a few hundred yards. On such evenings as this, that can be journey enough.

We cross the field, sweet with blooming grasses, our shadows long before us. Let us sit here amid the ruddy sheep sorrel and the chickweed stars and the fleabane opening lavender and bleaching white.

Crane flies rise from the blades. Pistons of limned gnats rise and fall as far as we can see toward the sun, sinking now behind the old maple on the hilltop, bristling with gold.

I brush a mosquito from your hair. Summer, indeed.

We hear from beyond the hill the gasp of tires on asphalt. We hear a train whistle in the Cassellman Valley five miles away. There is moisture in the air, sound travels well, rain later.

We hear the rush of a jet, a missile at the point of a chalky lance. Contrails converge in the west. Suspended by its parachute, a dandelion seed floats by, bigger than the jet and certainly more real. The world is a busy place.

The birds sing deeper in the woods now. The peepers begin. Only the crickets seem unaffected by the approach of night, their song unchanged.

How well we know these weeds that surround us, the goldenrod and the wild sunflower, knee-deep and not half grown. We can almost hear the hum of life that will swarm about their flowers come late July.

We find comfort in knowing the land. Place wisdom, we've heard it called.

A gibbous moon and a single star — a planet, Jupiter, we think — rise from the trees at our backs and climb in the violet east.

The windows of the house glow yellow, brighter now than the sunset which has been unspectacular, a moment of gold, a blanket of magenta spread over the blue hills and striped by purple clouds. Unspectacular is good, we say, for it means the air is clean.

The birds grow silent. The peepers grow loud. A chorus of bullfrogs embarks on a plangent madrigal.

We hear a woman's voice, calling children in. "It's dark!" she calls.

As the children know, only those inside would think it dark.

There is light enough to see the tufts of dandelions, light enough to shine on the faces of birch leaves, light enough to see the silhouettes of bats feeding at the treeline where we sit.

Up and down the field they fly, diving and tipping and picking off mosquitoes by the hundreds as they drift out of the woods. I throw my cap into the air, and a bat follows it down, so close we hear it chatter.

It is a Maxfield Parrish sky, brightest at the horizon, a dome steel blue descending in the west. Sometimes you can feel this old earth roll.

No, it is not dark. And now there is the moon, and now our shadows lie again upon the grass.

Sit and listen to the songs of night. The stars join us. Stay.

Free for the Hefting

Minimalists love found things. Take this chair, for example. I did. I took it from a heap of old furniture piled on a loading dock and destined for the junkyard.

When I picked it up, I understood why an otherwise perfectly good office chair had been scrapped. Heft this chair six or eight times, surround yourself with a gaggle of bulb-tanned narcissists watching themselves flex in the mirrored wall, and you could call it a workout.

I'm trying to say the chair is heavy.

Still, it's a great chair. Steel-framed, bead-welded, bolted and riveted, this chair was made to last. My guess is that is has outlived the productive careers of at least two generations of office workers.

Sit on the leatherette cushion and feel the impression of the haunches that have toiled here before you. We are all built pretty much the same, really. Even the wool stuffing removed by the mouse that chewed through the bottom has only made the seat more comfortable.

This morning I carried this chair to the edge of the runaway field, puffing from the effort, careful not to sprain my back, and now I rest on it, looking out across the green slope.

Tree swallows return to the nest box behind me every 30 seconds or so where a young one waits with its head out. Both parents work at catching insects, one close to the grass and one higher up, and higher still a red-tailed hawk turns beneath the curdled clouds. Ah, the world is a kinder place from a comfortable chair.

I prefer the worn, the well-used, the humanized. In a tattered workshirt, softened to the point of decay, I sit typing on an old Smith-Corona, enjoying the deep stroke and the satisfying rapping of the keys and the phrases streaming toward the left. (The whir and the heat of the computer have driven me from the office.) I enjoy the sound of the wind in the lifting boughs.

This typewriter, too, is a found thing. I found it at a yard sale.

No one wanted it.

"I called the business machine store to find out what I should ask for it," my mother said.

"The man told me to throw it in the dumpster. He said they take them on trade-ins, but just throw them out. No market for them."

I was incredulous. A perfectly good writing machine, trash. I am tempted to travel the countryside adopting abandoned manual typewriters, picking them up for the lifting, just as you could do years ago with upright pianos.

A guy I knew in a previous life kept 20 old uprights in his barn. Seated at many of them were undraped manikins he had hauled away from a department store, all free for the taking. Some were playing, some couchant on one elbow on top, a few even seated high on the beams, one or two peaking out from the hay mow.

This guy, too, loved found things. How I envy him the space.

This chair I had stored for a decade in the stable, upside down on the dirt floor. I hosed it off, wiped it down, and set it up. I oiled the swivels and pivots. It is perfectly good, just like this typewriter, and just right for sitting at the edge of the field with the fleabane nodding at your back and the swallows dipping, and your toes in beaded clover, just right for barefoot writing.

I will take care of it now, as I will this typewriter, that it may serve the next person who values it. Such a view, broadly held, would benefit the earth.

Not everyone, I know, shares my passion for found things. I once stumbled upon a perfectly good cashmere scarf discarded by an overzealous reveler outside the main lodge of a ski resort. After a good soaking and sterilizing, I knew it would be soft and warm. A companion failed to see the value, however, and stalked off, appalled that I was crawling around in the bushes for a scarf fouled with chunks.

I laugh at the memory, swiveling in this chair. I rise and turn it over. SIT-WELL. Remington-Rand of Buffalo and New York. I admire its superstructure — hammered steel and 3/16ths plate. I find gum, tucked away by a right-handed person, perhaps at a supervisor's approach.

Anyone with money can buy a new chair. This one has history. It suits me.

All-Day Rain

Wet, dismal days have always pleased me. Perhaps some ancient Irish preference for soft weather lives in me. Perhaps I tend toward melancholy. Whatever the reason, I am moved by the peaceful cleansing of the air and earth, by the nurturing of life.

We need rain in Upper Turkeyfoot. On such a hot, dry day as this, with the earth cracking on the hilltop and the dust rising from the road, I write of rain to please myself, to offer small relief, to prime the pump.

Your senses tell you; you need no forecast. Yesterday you saw the crenelated sky, the curdled clouds, and now you hear the whistle of the train soughing in the valley.

And you know: Rain coming.

The wind picks up. It lifts the leaves of maples bordering the field, moves through the trees in silver waves. The storm appears, high and bright, thumping in the west. The air turns yellow.

The dogs come panting to the porch; the chickens file into the coop; the horses trot toward the stable, manes flying in the sudden chill.

You climb the hill and watch it come. Black vapors boil overhead, roiling like ink in water, but in the west the sky is flat, smoothed by rain that falls in curtains, great riffling sheets advancing toward you over the hills.

Those first big drops hit hard, hard and cold against your back. And then the rush of rain, sweeping over the house and yard, exploding in waves on the tin roof of the coop.

On the porch you hold your hand beneath the eaves and let the water splash against your palm. Off the roof it rolls. It slaps against flat stones. It leaps from puddles and from the pond in a hundred-thousand crystal spires.

Lightning partitions the sky, rivers of blinding energy that make men face fate and children chatter. How far away was that one?

The rain keeps on — the maple trunk nearest the porch grows dark and veined with water, each rivulet pulsing with the rhythm of the storm — then eases some, then stops.

Lightning stutters deep in the even gray, softened by distance, thumping in the east, thumping like the beating of your heart.

You step into the chill and walk the shining woods. The sky reflects in every stone and leaf. Water drips from tier to tier, runs down trunks in black streaks, sudses at the mossy roots.

You hear a crumpling of sky, close by, above the gleaming canopy of green. You cross the field and head for home.

Runoff fills the pasture spring. Ignoring the turns and dips, it slides straight down the slope toward the barn, flattens the long grass, and pulls along a train of bubbles that spin in eddies and vanish in folds. Calves come to watch, snorting through pink muzzles.

A sodden moth struggles to reach the shelter of the pines. Branches droop from walnut trees, their leaves cutting patterns of herringbone in the twilight mist.

Thunder snaps like a rifle shot, and the rain begins again, a cool dripping in the dark, dripping in the trill of insect night.

You go to bed, and still the storms roll by, building and fading and building again. The room shows blue in pops of eerie light. Thunder shakes you from sleep, stepping you toward sunrise.

The last wave passes. The dogs, curled against the doorstep, sleep easier now. As do you. You sleep the deep and peaceful sleep sustained by miracles.

The Legs Go First

Practice is over. The pitcher and the shortstop stretch out on the bleachers, leaning back on their elbows, propping their heels on the plank below, agreeing that the legs are the first to go.

Everyone else has left. Their caps, where the bill meets the crown, are dark with sweat. The knees of their jeans are yellow with the dirt of the infield.

"The arm feels good," the pitcher says, rotating his shoulder, the nylon of his jacket singing.

"Real good. Only threw two or three as hard as I could. A fella could go three innings that way." He grins, teeth framed by beard.

"That's the first curveball I've seen in 20 years," says the shortstop, amazement in his voice. "Twenty years!"

He rubs his knee that he had wrapped with elastic after work where dreams of lining a shot into the gap had carried him through the afternoon.

The ballfield spreads out before them, empty, desolate.

They are fathers. They are coaches. And this evening, for a few minutes, they are players once more. Will be, while they stay.

Five had showed. Just five. It was to be a contest of the generations, a chance for men at mid-life to summon dormant skills, to show what once they were. Nothing to lose, they figured. Should be fun, they said.

They loosened their arms, these five, the pop of leather against leather reviving memories of glory in the dirt. They short-hopped the low ones with a casualness that comes from years on the field. They stooped for grounders hit by their sons who hooted when their fathers erred.

"Keep your glove down!" the sons yelled, reveling in reversed roles. "Charge the ball!" they jeered.

The fathers laughed and worried, suddenly, about their pride.

The wives had arrived in separate cars, and when they realized no one else would come, they watched their stars take batting practice before they left.

"Nice rip!" the men encouraged each other. They complained about the sound of the aluminum bats, but were happy to make contact. Even popups inspired awe.

"You got it! You got it!" they called, and the ball smacked the packed earth just beyond an outstretched glove.

"Ah, he woulda had it 10 years ago!"

They took turns pitching, mocking each other's curveballs, whooping at speared liners.

On the mound, his loose workshirt heavy with sweat, the pitcher signaled a curve with a flip of the wrist, then served up a heater, high and tight.

The shortstop hit the deck. He picked himself up and slapped sawdust from his pants.

"You coulda killed me," he said.

Everyone laughed. Only players would find this funny. And they were players.

From the bleachers now they look out across the field. A swirl of yellow dust races from third to second. The backstop casts long shadows.

"I spent a lot of innings out there on that mound," the pitcher says. "A lot of innings."

The sun drops behind the school on the hill where all-terrain vehicles climb the slope, engines droning in the distance.

"Seemed like we were always playing ball. Every chance we got. Never saw the field empty like this. What is it today? I don't know."

A red three-wheeler bursts from the trees behind them, corners sharply with one tire off the ground, and roars into the outfield. The driver is incredibly young, a wisp of a boy under a massive, gleaming helmet. Five, maybe.

They watch in silence. The pitcher flexes his arm. "It feels real good," he says.

Wanting Less

It took a while to relax.

I felt guilty wasting time. So much to do. Checks to write, contracts to finalize, grass to mow. Deadlines and commitments.

Yet it had been months (is it possible?) since I had walked in the woods, weeks since I had simply watched the evening bloom.

Amid the clutter of the back porch I stood looking out across the grass gone to seed, listening to the sibilation of damp wind in the woods beyond the field, watching the slow undulations of the trees, pelagic. I have always been struck by the sameness of the ocean and the forest.

I stood there looking out from amid the clutter and the concerns to which I saw no end. They would keep, I decided. Into the field I hurried before the telephone rang again. I needed this.

The sun made its first appearance of the day, and the world was varnished with rain.

Steam drifted up from the wooded valley. Crows rose from knee-deep corn. Into the ripening oats I waded, following the narrow path inadvertently left by the farmer, an empty row filling now with nutgrass and ragweed.

American coppers fluttered above the grain, and my passage disturbed sulphurs that spun into the sky in pairs, tracing double helixes through the heavy air.

And here, at the edge of the field, a deer had lain, perhaps this very afternoon, the young goldenrod flattened to thatch against the wet and ticking earth.

On this wild hilltop bed I stood, pantlegs soaked and sticking to my thighs. I looked back upon the house, small among the hills and ridges of these Laurel Mountains, diaphanous in mist, small beneath the clouds.

Americans, I have read, are working more hours now than at any time since before World War II. We want "The Good Life" and are willing to sweat for it.

We want cellular phones in our European cars. We want central air conditioning in our summer homes. We want vacations so frenetic we return exhausted. We want. We want.

Yet what "The Good Life" really means to us, what we really want, is to relax, to kick back free from care, if only for an evening.

Standing in the oats, looking down upon the house and the concerns of my life, I realized that getting what we really want is a luxury easily afforded. I had forgotten. We have world enough and time.

In the woods, deep hoofprints of deer punctured the sodden loam. Wind crawled through the treetops, and the rain visited again. Cardinals squalled over territory, fighting with song.

There exists a peace here I find nowhere else—the good life, easily afforded. Here, I have it made.

Yes, I need it, as do you. We should treat ourselves more often.

Influences of Evening

Such plans we had. But let us try to put aside, for now, our fears and our regrets. Let us try.

Beside the pond, let us resign ourselves to the influences of evening. The birds are singing in their roosts among the trees that hide the old farm road. The sun has already sunken in the mist, and the few, high wisps of cirrus turn salmon overhead. Yes, we shall try.

Bullfrogs leap into the dark water at our approach; with a glump and a splash they complain of our presence.

Let us sit here on the newly planked dock, the sour smell of oak in our nostrils, the nails just beginning to stain the wood, the dark water around us, the cattails swaying silently in the rising wind.

A half moon brightens. We see it twice. On the water it is close enough to touch. It shatters when we do. Is there something here for us, something to restore our dreams?

The frogs begin to surface, accepting us with their brassy eyes and yellow grins. There is magic in the water. Its dimensions change — now deep as sky with the moon reflected there, now broad as a continent with trees inverted on the rim, now thin as a window between worlds when a tadpole breaks the surface for a gulp of air.

The birds go quiet, and we can hear the crickets now. A farmhand shouts a mile away, and it sets the dogs to barking.

The moon is the color of marigolds. A robin is the last to sing. A frantic column of midges drifts out of the reeds on a rising breeze. We see it indistinctly, and only when we look away. A bird swoops by. Impossible to identify in the evaporating light, it darts back and forth over the surface of the water. A bat! Of course! There's another, feasting on the insects rising from the wetland.

The land goes black. No longer can we see the bales in the field. Only sky and water hold their sheen, and now we see Jupiter in both.

To those inside their homes, perhaps dining under incandescence or staring at their flashing televisions, it is dark outside. The blackness presses against their windows. But not for you and me. Against the sky and water we can see the blades of cattails, the crowns of trees, the flight of bats, each other. We have been here to greet the night, and we are part of it.

Great events are happening above us we know — a comet slamming into Jupiter. Great events are happening, too, on this planet — great tenors singing together, a nation celebrating the World Cup.

Yet here at this pond, the bullfrogs are as astonishing as Domingo, Carerra and Pavorotti. Here, too, we feel cause for celebration, here in the present.

We are restored. Nature has done its work on us.

As James Cozzens has written, when we think of the past we regret, and when we think of the future we fear. But there is the present to think of, and as long as we live, there will always be.

Our eyes are open. Our world intact. In the present, every day is a miracle.

It is night. In the dark it is difficult to tell where heaven ends and earth begins. It is easy to believe there is no difference.

Fireflies lead us home.

Hair of the Dog

More beige. I need more beige: Clothes and furniture and cars and rugs. Especially rugs.

Bob Murphy, you see, is beige. Bob is our dog. Our big dog. Our big, beige, shedding dog.

(At this point I wish to apologize to Mrs. Bob Murphy of Johnstown who wonders why I didn't give Bob "a real dog's name, like Fido or Rover." We considered calling "Costas" because he has a penchant for histrionics, but too late. He's licensed and on the county books. Mrs. Murphy, I hereby grant you permission to get a dog and name it Jeff O'Brien.)

I'm not sure why Bob is shedding. Me, who has shed his last, hasn't a clue.

Maybe it's the heat. Maybe he's nervous. Maybe he's allergic to the geese that live beside the lake across the road. Whatever, the reason, he's losing hair at an alarming rate.

Amazing, the amount of hair on a Labrador. Not long, just thick, so thick Labs can climb out of the lake, shake once, and be dry. Bred to leap into the cold North Atlantic and retrieve nets, they have this special underlayer of fur, an under layer that is fast becoming an overlayer on everything in this house rougher than chrome. If ever I forget to put the car in park and it drifts into the lake, the back seat, Bob's seat, will remain as dry as a bone.

It collects in balls under the desk. It sticks to the bottoms of my running shoes. It adds texture to my navy blazer. The irony is not lost on me — me, the nations's baldest columnist wearing the hairiest jacket.

Last winter I bought this great cashmere topcoat. Got it on sale at the outlet center. Wore it to town for an important meeting, feeling debonair.

"Dog at home?" the attorney asked, smirking.

I clean it up, daily. I vacuum the furniture. I empty the bags. Blessed with hardwood floors, I slide it all into a beige heap with a dust mop, compress it in my fist, and drop it in the the garbage. It is warm. An excellent insulator, I should save it to fill the walls between the studs. It wouldn't take long. Or maybe bag it and give it to the Amish for stuffing quilts. Throw them in the wash, one shake, and they're dry.

Some of it, I believe, is the exact density of air and hangs forever suspended in the household atmosphere, waiting to be inhaled.

When I roll down the windows on the interstate, its sets up a beige flurry in the cockpit. How would I explain that one?

"Sorry for weaving, officer, but I was nearly unconscious from holding my breath."

My eyes have been watering a lot lately. Excuse me while I sneeze.

Listen. I'm open to suggestions. We scrambled Bob some eggs. We bathe him monthly with baby shampoo. Would Vidal Sassoon help? I brush him every two days. Fur balls roll through the yard like tumbleweeds.

Heavy rain slaps against the side of the house as I write. I've been shaking the dust mop out the front door. I expect a beige clog to back up the storm sewers. Easily traced, I risk a fine from the town fathers. Having spent all our cash on Miracle Brushes and sweeper bags, I would be forced to walk down Market Street in a hair shirt.

If Bob loses all his fur, the wife suggests we become an attraction and charge admission like Indian Caverns on the way to State College, erecting signs every mile or so along the highway: Bald Man and his Bald Dog, 7 miles ahead. Now, there's an idea — hair systems for dogs.

Meanwhile, I'm in the market for a beige couch. I might trade the car this week, looking for something with a tan interior.

Not to worry. Sometimes the best action is no action. Left alone, everything will be beige soon enough.

Storm Coming

The wind visits. The tablecloth on the clothesline moves white in the dark like a night spirit. The dogs whimper in their pen. Storm coming.

We have been waiting. We have stood on the hard earth with the heat rising around us and looked skyward, searching for rain sign, finding none, waiting for the common miracle.

The half moon first showed pink as the sun dropped into the mist behind the hills, then darkened to orange as the day drained into the west.

Clouds flooded the deepening sky, and the moon showed through them, nebulous and rusting as the clouds thickened and the first flashes of light fluttered in the sky, silent flashes without thunder.

Now the moon is hidden. Now the sky jumps with light. Now thunder spills overhead like a bushel of apples overturned on a tin roof.

When the thunder stops, we hear the rasp of cicadas. Wind walks through the woods beyond the field, now it hisses effervescent in the pear tree by the house. In the stuttering blue light, we see the boughs sway.

Thunder rolls in from a long way off, rumbles across the pulsing sky like wagon wheels on a plank bridge. The radio in the kitchen mentions lightning over Three Rivers Stadium 60 miles away. The Pirates have tied it up. But we are occupied by more important things.

The rain begins. It runs off the porch roof and slaps against the stones. The dog curls up against the door. Pears fall; we hear them hit the ground.

Lightning rips and booms, no longer separated from its thunder. Ragged, it loops from cloud to cloud. It hurts our eyes. It shoots straight down behind the hill.

It doesn't last long. The rain eases, no longer billowing off the roof. Only a steady, fine shower through which moths fly. Only the cool, sweet air. Only the grass sparkling in the light escaping from the house.

We step inside. The weatherman shows us radar images of the storms advancing at 30 mph. He warns of heavy downpours, of flash flooding. The wind moves through the screen and joins us in the living room. The rain begins again.

All night the storms roll over us, wave after wave like breakers on the beach, the pattern repeating — the wind rising and the sky flashing and the thunder catching up to the lightning and the rain slapping down.

"We do need the rain," the weatherman had said with a scowl. "But this intensity is ridiculous!"

What is ridiculous, it seems to us, is to expect nature to be anything but intense. We want the storm to nourish our selfish and myopic lives at our convenience, like our tamed beasts, like our machines. We want control.

Too long removed from the natural world, we exaggerate our own importance. When so ordinary a thing as a thunderstorm reminds us that we are far from supreme, it surprises us, and we pout like scolded children.

Our bedroom, too, had jumped with light all night, and we are up later than usual. We walk the sopping yard, steaming coffee cup in hand.

The clothesline has snapped, and the tablecloth lies heavy on the grass. Chairs are overturned. Pears litter the ground. The pond is brown and viscous with silt. Frogs peek out bright green. The hayfield is flattened in swirls. We see the storm's footprint. We praise what matters most.

Night Farmers

Rain falls in Upper Turkeyfoot, warm and slanting from the east, sure to raise the worms.

Tonight, just after dark, we should slip on our duck shoes, grab the flashlight we keep by the door, and sit beside the garden to watch the worms emerge.

But, oh, the rain. Step off the porch and turn your face into it, easy and steady and so rare this past month it seems even more of a miracle. Farmers in the Midwest call this a lady rain, the best kind, life-giving.

It eases some, falling so lightly that it does not soak through our jackets even though we can see it against the dark woods.

Everything looks better in the rain, Thoreau wrote, and so it does. The forest has a tropical feel with ferns as high as our waist and wild bergamot in bloom and air thick with mist. Under the dripping canopy we walk in even light, the day diffused. We cast no shadow.

Even in the stinging nettles do we see beauty, so long as our bare legs don't brush against them, the broad, toothed, leaves varnished and reflecting tin sky.

And tonight, if we're lucky, we'll watch the earthworms come up. They go deep in dry weather such as we've had, sometimes as deep as eight feet, but usually 18 inches or so.

Worms, you say? O'Brien wants to talk about worms? What happened to the purple prose? Ah, if you would have been with me after such a rain one night in June, you might understand. Let me tell you about it.

The rain stopped in failing twilight. In the vapor and the dusk, I went to check the garden. The tilled earth was moving, an undulation barely perceptible, yet the effect was unsteadying, and I felt a mild vertigo as if I were suddenly at sea. The worms were rising.

First a clump of earth would shift, perhaps a leaf would lift, and an earthworm would appear, its head wagging in the damp air, touching the ground here and there, searching for food. Feeding, they stretch themselves full length, 10 inches or more, their tails always anchored in their holes where they will retract with astonishing speed and strength if touched.

They lie maybe four to each square foot of garden. They eat just about anything, leaves, flowers, raw meat, and most importantly of all, earth.

Ingesting soil from beneath the surface, the worm grinds it in its gizzard filled with grains of sand which act as millstones. In its stomach it adds lime (unique among animals), then excretes refined soil onto the surface from its tail, casting the digested earth left and right, building the small towers we'll find in the morning if we look.

The entrance to its burrow is lined with leaves, grasses, flowers. It will bury bones and twigs. Thus the earthworm plows, harrows and fertilizes the land.

Darwin estimated that more than 50,000 worms inhabit an acre of land and that the whole superficial layer of vegetable mold passes through their bodies every few years at a rate of 18 tons an acre yearly.

Stars and fireflies may provide the show on a summer night, but earthworms do the work. You must admit, there is wonder in that.

Cardinals announce an end to the rain. Light drains into the west. Let us take our torches and sit beside the garden. At our feet, worlds exist we never knew.

Hey. An old editor taught me decades ago: If you start purple, finish purple.

Corn Day

Friend, you say you feel the signs of summer's end — the robins flocking, the katydids sawing in the thousand-noted night, the asters blooming in the brittle field. I feel them, too. Easily panicked, we race about to make the season last.

Each spare moment has been scheduled. So much to do. Picnics and fairs and shopping shall occupy our days. Then school begins, and summer ends. But does it?

What fools we are to rush the seasons. We notice the changes around us, and we mistake them as endings. They are not, of course, for time is cyclical, and circles have no ends.

What we feel today are the signs of summer's peak. Toward this fullness has our world been striving, and it is with us now, ripe summer, and we are in it. Let us go and walk the fields and woods and know it to be so.

Slowly. Life was meant to be lived slowly.

Let us dare to be still for one hour under the sky. Let us do nothing but sit and, in the company of our own thoughts, feel the world around us, feel the day expand. Let us match our rhythms to the season.

Come with me if you would. Let us go now, while the cows sing in the haze and the sunflowers swing their heavy heads toward the south.

The dog slaps her tail on the porch when we open the back door, but she does not get up. How long her day must seem. Through deep grass we walk. Cabbage moths and honey bees cruise the clover.

With the sun warm upon our necks we cross the gravel road and skirt the pond, heading for the cornfield. Dragonflies patrol the pond's edge, their wings backlit and flashing like oil on water. Winged grasshoppers launch themselves before us; out of the hay stubble they clatter in clumsy, short flight. Crows move down the treeline, squawking at our presence.

Here in the tall grass and goldenrod between the pond and the field, the crickets are in full chorus. We hear the trill of August.

We have come to the edge of the cornfield, a wall of green ten feet high. The day heats up. Cicadas whir. Between the stalks we see the cool and shaded rows, the leaf-draped aisles. We can't resist.

Sideways we brush between the stalks. One, two, three rows deep we wade, more. We lose count, immersed in green and shadows.

Let us sit here on the packed earth with the long blades arching over us and the tassels rising high into the starched blue sky. We do not speak. Green isolation.

We hear the steady rattle of the crickets and the sound of our own breathing. The wind rises. Through the corn it moves with the sound of rain. A ground beetle turns circles at our feet.

Shards of light fill this world beneath the blades. We feel them on our skin, these scraps of sunlight, and could trace their outline with our eyes closed. The wind comes again. This is a sound we cherish, wind in corn.

What plants are these! It is as if we see them for the first time: the magnificent ribbed leaves covered with fine hair, cupped and arched one over the other, in concert to catch the rain and the light; the stalks standing on bare roots as if on tiptoe; the splashes of burgundy amid the riot of green; the spires piercing the sky.

We share this spot with the sparrow we hear chirping nearby, and with the ladybird beetle searching for aphids on the underside of a leaf, and with the hoverfly whose feet feel wet on our skin.

The wind rises again, each rustle buoying us.

Time slows. It is summer now. This is miracle enough.

Card to my Wife

Greeting cards please you. I can see it in your face when the aide in her hospital greens enters your room with mail.

Here, then, is a card from home, written in the yard as the sun rises silver in the mist above the woods.

Read it from your bed with the window blind raised. Revel in that patch of sky, all you can see of the natural world, cropped and confined by the hard corners of the buildings that tower around you. From Upper Turkeyfoot I send a few minutes of morning as it happens.

A catbird mews in the lifting fog. Crows call to each other from their hilltops. Red squirrels chatter in the hemlocks, annoyed by the cat who stalks the damp shadows.

The night, Thomas Wolfe wrote, has a thousand voices. In September they continue unabated into day, a constant rattle and whir, crickets and cicadas and katydids and passing bees. In the country, if you listen, you know this is not the Age of Man, but the Age of Insects.

Swallowtails hang on the Joe-Pye weed I let grow in the perennial garden because it wanted to be there, crowding out the Sweet William that did not. The native grew high and sturdy, and now it blooms, as tall as a man, neither perfumed nor brilliant, but sweet enough to attract butterflies.

How much easier it is to live in conformity with nature. We are learning. Knowing what is enough, that is wisdom.

The dog misses you. He lays his big yellow head on my thigh as I write. He looks me in the eye and puts his paw on my leg and, if I let him, he would climb into my lap, all 80 pounds of him. You would let him, he knows. I thump his muscled shoulder with the flat of my hand. I tell him you'll be home soon.

The dew falls even as I type, my note paper curls and goes limp. A single bead tips each blade of grass.

Fog lifts now from the field to reveal swallows feeding perhaps a hundred feet up. The pines beside the barn cast long shadows over me. The morning brightens, the light catching in the crystal dew, in my breath, in the wings of sparrows. Steam rises from the hay.

Chester passes in his dump truck. Old enough for Social Security, he makes a little money hauling firewood. He waves as he passes, slowing to raise less dust, probably headed for the campground in the valley.

On calm summer evenings we can sometimes smell the smoke from the fires made of Chester's wood. I raise two fingers and point to the log shed. He nods. In the next week or so — no rush — he'll back into the yard, take down the clothes line and raise the bed.

Time to clean the flue. Yes, so soon.

The field is browner than you remember, though the asters have yet to bloom. The leaves begin to change (the weakest boughs turn first), and the trees, as they do in spring, take on their individual hues, subtle in early September, but enough to distinguish themselves.

Sunflowers hang their heads, heavy with seed. Corn silk blackens. The blackberries gleaming at the edge of the woods taste cold and sweet.

And the field, the field — stem and spider line, bowing timothy and sagging thread, beaded with the dampness of morning that soaks through my pantlegs as I walk, and above it all, as far as I can see over the hilltop, hang the masterpieces of the orb weavers.

Breathe the scent of Queen Anne's lace, their centers spotted royally, each efflorescence as delicate as a snowflake, each tiny petal a dewcup.

Under the apple tree against the woods, that sheltered place you love so much, I look back toward the house at my path through the dew.

One set of tracks I see where there should be two, and soon.

Primal Sanities

I am grateful for the small events that form the day. Walt Whitman called them "primal sanities." These moments are why I keep a journal. Seemingly mundane when I record them, they acquire a vividness with time. First-hand observations have no equivalent. Years later, reading them is a joy. Here are a few from a decade ago.

LOVE

We wrestle on the living room rug, the boy and me, enjoying the smack of muscle against muscle, frame against frame. He rolls onto his back and lifts his knees to his chin.

"Hop on," he says, eager to test his growing strength at 11. "Go ahead, all your weight."

I ease myself onto his socked soles.

"Oof!" he says. " I pity a chair."

LIGHT

The frost that stands in shards on clover blossoms and drew its spiny arteries on the glass has loosened stems of locust and ash. Leaves fall in a steady shower as the sun clears the eastern hills. Their patter fills the woods. Through crystal shafts they float, brought down by force of light.

FRIENDS

Like most Penn State grads, football season addles his brains. That I have never been to Beaver Stadium he finds incredulous.

"You've got to come. We'll take the women, and we'll stay in a bed and breakfast, and it'll be great!"

"Okay," I say. Pitt fans, these days, demure. An hour later he calls back.

"It's all set. We have a babysitter, and we have reservations for Saturday night. The women can pack a cooler and we'll take thermoses so we can tailgate with the other 90,000 people who will be there." Sounds like fun.

"One more thing," he says.. "Do you know anybody who might have four tickets?"

SEASONS
Blackbirds, dark against the sky, swoop into the hollow in a gasp of wings, but do not land. They turn and climb and climb once more above the trees, their number arching upward as if of one mind, flashing when they turn like the lifting of maple leaves before rain, like the wave of a hand.

LUCK
"Dad!" she screams. Up the stairs I bound, loose tie flapping, fearing the worst.

"Dad!" she greets me in her doorway. "I won!"

"Huh?" heart pounding, music in the room behind her.

"I don't believe it. I dialed the number while I was curling my hair, and I got right through, and I won! I won!" Won?

"Yes! I won an audition for Wheel of Fortune! I talked to Quinn and Banana Don, and I won!"

Over gulped breakfast she forbids her brother to tell anyone beyond the seventh grade. So what does this mean, I want to know.

"It means I'll need a new wardrobe and a new hairstyle," she says. "Oh, I won!"

NIGHT
A solitary cricket deetles by the path. I walk without a lantern. Sunlight strikes a gibbous moon and drops, pale and spent, into the woods.

The trunks of maples, smooth sinews, take on a sheen as sensuous as a woman's leg in black hose. Claws scrape on bark.

INNOCENCE
The boy lies on the carpet as if staked out by Comanche for the blistering sun to do its work. He talks on the phone to a girl.

"There's a fly on the ceiling," he says. Then, "Yeah. What I like to do is burn ants with a magnifying glass. What do you like to do with ants?"

He has my charm.

PEACE
I stacked firewood before lunch, dodging the occasional slushball thrown by the boy from behind the chicken coop. The girl appeared at the second floor window and waved clutching her toothbrush, her face puffy with sleep.

I sit now in Whitman's "splendid silent sun." Dishes clatter in the sink.

The Gray Poet had listed them 130 years ago:

"The field of unmowed grass: serene-moving animals, teaching content; nights perfectly quiet; a walk undisturbed; a rural domestic life away from the noises of the world."

Primal sanities. And necessary. Know them as they happen.

Among the Orb Weavers

Standing over the coffeemaker, I see through the kitchen window the cobwebs in the field, and I know I will be late to the office this morning. Some things are just too important to miss.

The field bag and folding stool I hang on my shoulder and, steaming coffee in hand, I step into the bright air. Sunlight pours through the treetops. Doves call.

For such mornings as this do I leave the field unmowed. Nature has runs its course on these few acres. Diversity returns. Wonders abound.

The webs of the orb weavers, backlit and beaded with dew, luff in the cool eddies that move through this tangled garden of Queen Anne's lace, budding asters, and blooming goldenrod, a garden untended by man, and, to my eye, more beautiful for it.

The dew makes the webs visible, hundreds of them, shining like spun glass among the ochers and the fading greens of late summer. On some of the closest webs I see the dark shapes of their makers. So excited do I become that I wade in barefoot and set up my stool, the stems of clover between my toes.

These are the works of garden spiders, Argiopes as black and yellow as swallowtails. They have strung their nets vertically from the fescue and the timothy, working in the evening. They begin by climbing high and spinning out a line of silk on the breeze. When it sticks to another stalk, they reel it in, adding tension. Then across this line they crawl, doubling it, for from this bridge they will hang their scaffolding.

They work at first in silk that is neither adhesive nor elastic, then walk upon these lines to build their final spiral coated with a sticky fluid, trimming away the first spiral as they go. The radii remain dry, and it is upon these that the spider runs to tie up its victims.

Watching an orb weaver build its web fills me with the same sense of awe as watching the stars wheel across the heavens.

The spider I watch now waits at the center of its web, its claws upon the radii like a fisherman's finger upon his line, waiting for a strike. Absorbed in the moment, I am unaware of time. This is happiness.

It lasts but a few minutes, the field draped with crystal orbs and the light refracting on the silk. Then the sun tops the woods and evaporates the dew — you can watch it rise as mist into the immaculate sky — and the light moves down the stalks and penetrates the thatch, and the baking of another rainless day begins, drying the cobwebs to invisibility, leaving only the canopies of the grass spiders to hold the dew close to the ground.

The insect world awakens. A dragonfly clatters in the timothy, rises, darts away. Fritillaries and monarchs appear. A fly rockets past. Listen to the crickets and the crows.

A parade of jets begins from east to west, crossing under the Milky Way I know is still there. I have such faith. There is order in the universe. Of this I have no doubt.

The orb weavers tend their nets.

Creek Relief

The water is cold at first, but you get used to it. The sun is high and hot. There is no breeze. The sycamores and birches hang still over the stream.

It is travel season. Friends traverse the continent, vacationing. A few even cross the ocean. They need it, they say. They seek joy in existence. You have stayed behind, believing peace to be found closer to home.

The heat of afternoon has driven you from the house. Riding with the windows down offers scant relief, even with your cheek against the rubber and your hand an airfoil in the rush.

Ah, but the creek will cool you; you feel it as you drift into the valley and the engine dies and you hear the water flow.

You wear old tennis shoes for better traction on the black-green stones that lie beneath the surface. You wade in, blanket folded under your arm, your feet squishing in your shoes, and you find in the middle of the creek a rock big enough and flat enough to lie upon. You spread the blanket and stretch out to face the sky.

Here, clear water sliding around you, enveloped in a liquid rumble, you are removed from striving. Living becomes simple, easy. This is what you need.

Birds wheel above, disturbed from their stone perches in the flow by your loitering. Cedar waxwings they are by their orange wingtips and yellow-banded tails. Hear them lisp.

You stare into the creek searching for life. There, at last, flash minnows. Now that you have fixed their form in your mind, you see them everywhere, expectation fulfilled. This is what you need.

The hollow shell of a crayfish lies white against an olive stone submerged. A raccoon has feasted here, perhaps the very one whose tracks you saw along the bank.

And as you imagine its black hands groping under stones and the crayfish fleeing backward, a leaf floats by, returning you to the surface, a yellow blade riding the current, a reminder of change. The wind rises with the thought and carries across the braided stream the first sweet smell of autumn. It happens as you watch. This is what you need.

Flowers bloom at your back, flourishing in crevices. Scarlet cardinal flowers and saffron sneezeweed and tiger-spotted jewelweed shiver in the breeze.

A minnow jumps, two, three times, flipping where the sun hits the water. A damsel fly darts among among smooth stones, brittle wings clattering. A greenbottle fly rubs its front legs together on your faded denim.

This is what you need. This, and, if you're lucky, someone to share it with, perhaps a child, mud smeared on the back of her calf, sunlight precious in her hair, her songs mingling with the thousand chords of continuance.

Off the stone you slide. You lie back in the current and give yourself up to the creek, let it carry you along for a moment like the leaves.

It is an act of faith. In this channel of green and crystal, with birds tracing scallops from bank to bank against a silver sky, with leaves gleaming against the shadow of deep woods, you trust this creek, this life.

You have what you need.

Fall

Autumnal Equinox

Author's Note: One full day I spent wandering the fields and woods. It was a gift to myself. I answered no telephone, watched no television, heard no radio. I met no other person. I left the house with water and fruit in my daypack, armed with a good pair of binoculars, a hand lens, and a journal. Here, then, are the notes I made, inadequate though they are, offered in an attempt to pass that gift along.

* * *

Autumnal equinox. I celebrate by spending the day in the woods and fields. I reside in wonder.

A handful of wild sunflowers seeds I scatter in the field riffling tan with the fragile bones of timothy. I smell sweet goldenrod at its peak. I take in the beauty of asters. Dew soaks my pantlegs.

In the woods I pause under an old apple tree I did not know existed, noting the depression where a deer had slept in the soft, dark humus where mushrooms grow. The wind breathes in the green canopy overhead. Cherry leaves tumble through the cool, damp air. An apple hurtles down and smacks the earth. Summer surrenders to gravity.

Knee deep in lady ferns, I hear the drumming of a grouse from farther up this wooded slope. Another step, and up it flies, buffeting the air as it rockets through the boughs.

The wind dies. Clouds seem suspended in the milky sky. Crickets and locusts sing. A hover fly looks me in the eye.

I spread my coat on wild strawberry plants in this field reverting to woods. Turkey vultures drift over. One turns its bare, red head as it passes.

The world reveals itself by degrees. A grasshopper climbs a stem of goldenrod as bees work the blooms. A locust borer crawls upon my hand. I am surprised to find myself looking at a katydid, leaf green and still, inches from my face. A catbird mews in the trees.

The dew has lifted and hangs in the sky as haze. The sun warms me; I feel its energy through my pantlegs. Brown ants inspect this page.

I climb the hill, filling my pockets with acorns. The groundhogs have been cleaning out their woodland burrows, preparing their hibernaculums. Acorns fall steadily. Crows clamor in the hollow. They chase an owl — no, a hawk. Through the glasses I see its rufous tail and speckled back.

The sun has set. A sphinx moth hovers at a dandelion gone to seed and shivering in a weak breeze as the valleys fill with mist and the ridges fade blue and the sky turns copper and the katydids saw.

I am still, still until the hills and sky become one and leave the distant lights of men to hang in space, still until the farmer cutting corn a mile away turns off his tractor, still until the haze settles once more upon the ground, upon me, still until the stars appear in the deepening sky, until I cast a shadow in the light from half a moon, still until the clover drips with dew.

I see taillights flow upon the road and hear the gasp of tires. I see winglights flash among the stars and hear the growl of jets. How little is known by traveling, how much by sitting still.

Contentment is easily found once we stop seeking it. I leave this hilltop wanting less, having found much more.

I walk toward the house, each step a joy. The screech owl cries again. The acorns fall.

Football in the Fall

Jerry Brophy sits in the shade of the tool shed with the bottoms of his trousers rolled and his feet in a pan of water.

Across the yard, the extended family piles food on picnic tables. He watches.

"This arthritis has got me down," he says, rubbing his pallid shins. "Those old football injuries have my legs all locked up."

An electric fan, propped aslant on a pile of scrap lumber and aimed in his direction, vibrates feebly.

"Ah," he says. "This feels terrific."

His skin is thin and translucent over the bones of his face. He cannot stand without help. His legs grow weaker each day.

Lou Gehrig's disease is killing Jerry Brophy.

His long limbs have thinned since last I saw him. His hand shakes now as he pours coffee from a thermos thoughtfully placed in the grass beside his chair. (It saves trips. Plus, you know how a man likes to do for himself.)

But he sits erect, a plaid cap of the type favored by the children of the Great Depression, by the sons of immigrants, cocked rakishly on his head.

And when he talks of football, you can see the light in his eyes. When he talks of football, he sees a long way off.

"They came and got me off the sandlot," he says. "Every town in the valley had a team in those days.

"They came and got me and told me I'd make a good center. Said they'd pay me, too. I told 'em, 'Hell, I'm no center. I'm an end. Been an end all my life.'"

Adults seat themselves under an umbrella sprouting from the middle of the table and make room for their plates among the salad bowls, cubed fruit in Tupperware, liters of cola. The children have a table of their own where they eat with their fingers and make faces, oblivious and blessed.

"So they put me at end. The other team had new uniforms and helmets. They took one look at us and laughed." He laughs himself at the memory.

"They hollered, 'Hey! We're gonna teach you coal miners a lesson!'" He grins and winks and tugs on his cap.

"I caught two touchdown passes, we beat 'em 45-0. I played end ever since."

He stares into the middle distance. He rubs his knees. When next he speaks, you can barely hear him.

"Oh, man," he says.

Another sits beside him, and Jerry Brophy begins again. He finds the telling easier the second time.

"Came and got me off the sandlot," he says. "Said I'd make a good center. Hell. Been an end all my life."

He describes feats of strength and grace; he recites the poetry of youth, this man with his feet in a dishpan and his trousers rolled.

Lou Gehrig's disease attacks the muscles by degrees. In the final stages, you cannot swallow. You suffocate.

Children run by in their swimsuits, laughing and trailing towels.

"Ah, to be a kid again," he says. "When you're a kid, you don't think anything can ever happen."

The sun drops behind the trees and casts long shadows on the pool. His wife helps him to his feet and supports him as he moves toward the car with short, halting steps. He is a tall man, and she fits easily under his arm.

She rejoins the family to offer thanks.

"It's his first time out since the hospital," she says. "He's very tired. He just told me that before today he felt half dead, but now he feels half alive."

Jerry Brophy sits alone in the back seat. The family says goodbye through the open window. Handshakes. Kissing. The car backs down the driveway. Waving.

They walk back into the yard, together. The children whoop and leap into the pool. Their parents and grandparents sit in silence, thinking of those things that last. Most stay later than they had intended.

A Happy Poverty

It seems so simple from here, so obvious.

I'm sitting in the barn, watching the rain fall, a steady, soaking rain, the kind farmers hoped for in July, too late now to help the corn, but just in time to ruin the last hay crop.

I have swung open the big doors to let in the soft light. Inside the barn, it has the quality of powder. I sit on a litter of loose straw on the plank floor, my back against a chestnut post. Through my jacket I feel the mark of the adze.

The sky is a wash of gray, almost silver, framed by the corrugated roof where the rain taps and by the dark, unpainted siding, and sectioned into shards by the compound leaves of the ash tree that rises through the fence boards.

In this cool dampness, I am content. All day I could sit here, cultivating a happy poverty.

I am learning how little it takes to sustain me.

This morning I fixed a lamp. Years ago it cost me a dollar at a flea market. I liked its marble base and tarnished stem. I liked its dented brass. I liked the signs of use.

(I confess, as well, to a particular weakness for worn books, the spines darkened by the palms of readers, a spot on the covers napped by thumbs.)

The socket where the bulb screws in had loosened, and the switch was unreliable. I took it apart. I cut back the brittle wire to where the rubber remained pliant, stripped the insulation, twisted the bright copper strands into loops and hooked them over the screws in the direction of their tightening. I reshaped the socket cover and refitted it into the base. It snapped together tight and good as new.

A simple chore, a job well done, and though no more complex than the trimming of the wick in an oil lamp, it gave me satisfaction.

I will never need another lamp. I could live out the rest of my days and never spend another dollar on one.

The Amish have a saying: "Use it up, wear it out, make it do, or do without."

That, to me, makes abundant sense.

The same can be said for most of what I need to live simply. I will never need another shirt, another coat, another shovel. I own my land. My pickup will last another 100,000 miles — more than I care to travel.

I have what I need.

My banker, I fear, would disagree. But do not measure me by net worth. (Better yet, do not measure me at all.) Besides, the Taoists believe possessions are yours only until someone takes them away.

I have this old house, sound enough for winter once I tar the flashing and glaze the storm windows.

I have my old books and a few people whom I love. A few are enough.

I have this barn where I can sit and listen to the rain on the roof, watch it slant across the field, hear it hiss in the trees.

Everything looks better in the rain. I love the sheen it gives to the ash leaves, to the rusted iron hinge, to the flattened grasses of the field, to the backs of my hands. It puddles at my feet, and I see sky there.

I begin to understand that what I need surrounds me, and I could pass the remainder of my seasons close to home and never yearn for more. The soul, Emerson stubbornly insisted, is no traveler.

So I sit on the barn floor and watch the rain, watch the clumps of asters bow with the weight of it, hear it tapping on the roof, feel the damp east wind that finds me in the powdery light.

This is not about an economy of money, but of time. It occurs to me that I have enough. I do, if I understand what is true wealth.

I will sit here until the chill penetrates my clothes. I will go inside, throw a log on the fire, and read by the light of an old lamp. Come morning, I will take pleasure in my work, in the rain if it lasts, in what I already have.

I wish you the same peace.

Soup, and How I Made It

The butcher wiped his big hands on his apron and shrugged.

"Sorry," he said. "No ham hocks. Just sold the last two. There's been a rush on ham hocks today. Must be the weather."

Must be. Frost had sparkled in the field when I awoke, morning glories hung limp on the coop, and a bumble bee lay trapped in a pane of ice on the dog's water bucket.

The first frost touches off a great scurrying. Chipmunks bark and squirrels race about. Walnuts fall and caterpillars bristle across the road. Each step in the field triggers a barrage of grasshoppers.

Humans feel it, too. There I stood before the butchers craving ham and bean soup.

"But I can cut you a nice piece of ham with a bone in it," he said. Okay by me, What did I know? I had never before made soup.

Though I am clumsy in the kitchen, I am still clever enough to know I needed a pot. A big one.

The grinning woman at Kitchen Collection listened politely as I explained my soup plans. I told her I wanted to make enough to give to friends. She helped me select a stainless steel caldron. Sixteen-quart. She must have thought me a very popular guy. Now that the soup has been produced and distributed, I would say I am less popular than I used to be. I filled the pot, dropped in the ham, added a bag of beans, turned the burner on low, and went to bed.

Day Two

The first thing I learned was that when you make 16 quarts of soup, you need more than one bag of beans and one hunk of ham. Even after I cut up the carrots and the onions and the cabbage and the potatoes, I could tell it needed more stuff.

I ground up a handful of pepper corns and dropped in a couple cloves of garlic. Still weak. Neither did Worcestershire help.

I put it on the porch to cool until I could get to the store the next day. The dogs ignored it.

Day Three

Twenty-four hours later I added another mound of ham and bone and dumped in a jar full of five different beans purchased at a Soroptimists' benefit.

In the freezer I found a block of green beans. It floated like a raft. I put the lid back on, watched Letterman, and went to bed.

Day Four

I awoke to the aroma of soup cooked to perfection. I turned off the stove and opened the windows.

That evening it was still warm. I ate two bowlfuls and pronounced it delicious. My father-in-law tasted the broth and seemed momentarily stunned.

"This would be good if you were really hungry," he said. I left the room and heard him and his daughter chuckling.

The soup had an immediate and dramatic effect. I slept alone.

Day Five

I filled old peanut butter jars with this delicacy of the season and presented them to friends. They inspected the beige pottage and managed to thank me. I ate two more bowls and suffered through a long night.

Day Six

I called around for reviews.

"Extremely unusual," said one. "My boyfriend said it has a delightful undertone. He's musical, you know."

"My husband thought I made it," said another. "I had to set the record straight before it wrecked our marriage."

And there was this one:

"I could explode at any moment."

Ah, well. Maybe I could offer the recipe to Lillian Vernon as a novelty item. She could list it on the same page with the hand buzzer and the whoopie cushion.

But, no. Methane contributes to global warming. This soup threatens the environment. I am filled with remorse.

A neighbor with her ear to the ground has let me in on a secret — ginger. She says it has a quieting effect. Now she tells me.

A Promise to Ourselves

We've been working hard, you and me. We wonder where the summer's gone, and the first touch of crimson in the maples fills us with longing.

Something is missing. Oh, we have had our successes. At work we make great strides. At home we plan for the next day. We are dedicated and capable. We even dare to think we deserve the respect of our peers.

But these are surely hollow triumphs for they leave us feeling empty. Something is missing.

This morning we stand in the yard under the lavender clouds and hear the walnuts dropping. We intend to sit in front of the computer, as is our routine. But wind rises in the locusts, and in a shower of tumbling leaves, we change our minds.

We have not walked to the cabin in awhile. Let us leave behind our mercenary impulses and walk the fields and woods in search of... in search of we don't know what.

Perhaps we might scare up a brood of grouse, bursts of wingbeats one after the other. Or maybe we will catch sight of the flock of wild turkeys we saw crossing the road last week, 50 blue heads bobbing as they ran.

But, no. Better to go expecting nothing, yet open to everything.

Bumble bees move among the asters. Goldenrod toss in the wind. At the top of the field we turn to look toward the valley and the echoes of crows. The ridges run blue, dissolving in the west behind the rain that will soon reach us.

We step into the peace of the woods. Sheltered from the wind, we leave behind insect rattle and horizons. Birch leaves lie yellow on the path.

In the sugar saplings we see all the colors of the coming fall, subtle now, but there nonetheless. In a few weeks people will gasp in wonder from their cars. How sad their smiles as they mourn change. Too fast, they'll sigh. Ah, but the change is neither fast nor slow; the seasons change gradually and continually.

Time speeds up only when we ignore it. Preoccupied with society and our place in it, we age in ignorance, caught up in the transitory. As the philosopher advised, it is good to remind ourselves every day that we will die. And when we get to the end of things, which is it we would rather do one more time, sit in front of the computer, or walk among the trees?

So let us just enjoy this afternoon.

The rain we saw in the valley now taps upon our backs as we reach the cabin. We prop the door and open the window. The air is rank with decay. On the pine we find the wreck of a mouse, a hull of fur and bones with the light showing through.

We sweep the floor. We build a fire. We burn our thumb on the stove door. We sit in the oak rocker and watch the orange, elastic flames. We read Emerson. Heat presses against our shins.

Our day seems full. In the small details of living we find the big assurances.

We could carry water from the spring down the slope. We could cook dinner on this stove, something dehydrated from packets under the iron bed. It would be enough.

It would be enough to gather sticks and carry water, to feed ourselves and hang our shirt near the stove to dry, to warm our joints before the fire, to fall asleep to the tremolo of owls and awake with the lace of leaves and sky in our eyes. It would be enough.

We will live closer to the earth. We will. We leave the trees and walk toward horizons.

No Walk in the Park

The runners were already on the course, having started 10 minutes ago, completing the first mile loop and huffing by with the wind in their hair, the showoffs.

"So," I thought, "That's what they look like," for, until today I had been one of them, galumphing along in the middle of the mob with, no doubt, that same scowl of intensity. How serious they looked.

But today I was a walker, and glad of it. Today, because of a pulled hamstring, I would sashay in the fall sunshine and enjoy the race, exchanging pleasantries with my straight-legged comrades.

Or so I thought.

This was new to me. At a walking clinic before the race, I learned about locking my knee under me, about leading with my chest, about pumping my elbows and swaying my hips, about gliding and "dropping."

"Dropping" is what you do with your pelvis as your leg locks under you. Master it, I'm told, and win trophies.

The female instructor demonstrated. She looked terrific swaying and dropping in her fuchsia shorts and shoes with matching accents. I tried it in my paint-splattered T-shirt and shoes with matching accents. I felt like an idiot.

These were unnatural movements for the male frame, it seemed to me, especially the hip stuff. But I was game. So what if I looked ridiculous, I'd give it a try. Besides, my running buddies would be miles ahead.

At the line they gathered, pressing against one another, bare shoulders touching, hearts pounding, breathing on each others backs.

The starter raised his pistol.

"Walkers!" he boomed, "Take your marks!"

Two hundred leaned forward as one, me among them, poised like a pack of pointers before a quail. And in that last moment before the gun, feeling a camaraderie with my fellow walkers as we grinned and wished each other luck, I knew that, at last, I had found my niche in the world of footracing.

Hey, this was going to be fun.

And, bang, we're off!

Pump sway lock drop, pump sway lock drop — I was in trouble here.

Already I could see my instructor flashing fuchsia a hundred yards ahead. Already sweat beaded on my noggin. Already I wheezed.

Pump sway lock drop.I felt like I was going to throw a wheel.

Oh, it's not that I was slow. I maintained my speed by ignoring pain. Most of the pack trailed me. I knew they were back there because I heard them yelling.

"You're running!" they called. "Runner!" they gasped in disgust.

But I was locking my knee. I was. I was trying my best.

A guy cruised up alongside and muttered something about fairness and the lack of judges on the course. He informed me I was "lifting," something about moving my bulk up and down when I should've been gliding. Easy for him, thin as he was. Me, if I were to glide any more the soles of my shoes would have burst into flames from the friction.

Still, I tried. I did. Near the end of the five kilometers I had no idea if I was locking and gliding or not, being numb from the waist down. Two guys bounced past, knees bent.

"Runners!" I growled. The scum.

Turned out, I won a medal. First in my age group. Bronze, with three men and a woman in mid-stride, all of them lifting. Maybe I was, too. I don't know. But I'm keeping my medal. I earned it, despite what they say.

It's lonely at the top.

Shorty Died

The family gathers rarely, and they are glad to see each other again.

But the reminiscing stops when the organ music starts, and they take their seats on the padded folding chairs to hear what the preacher has to say about Shorty.

He reads a lot of scripture, as preachers do. Then he lifts his head and tells a few stories.

"He always had time for me," the preacher says. "Once I asked him to take a look at an electrical outlet that had stopped working, and I found myself being trained as an electrician. 'Hand me this,' or, 'Hand me that,' he'd say,"

Yes, that was Shorty, people nod. It seems Shorty had repaired a lamp or wired a porch light at just about every house in town. The old ones poke the young ones with their canes. The smiles return.

Shorty's obituary took two columns in the local paper. Folks said they had no idea he'd done so much. Turns out, Shorty had written it himself.

"A 25-year member of Alcoholics Anonymous," it stated. Shorty wasn't one to brag, but that was important to him.

"Without that," he had said, "None of the rest could have been possible."

Maybe Shorty didn't dwell much on his accomplishments in Kiwanis or the Masons or the Presbyterian Church, but what he would talk about was his music.

He played the fiddle for 60 years, and he loved to tell about the days when he and his brothers would carry the furniture onto the porch, roll up the rugs, and play on the stairs at "house parties" while couples square-danced in adjoining rooms.

A tape exists made by a grandson. Shorty talks a little before each song.

"Here's one I learned from an old-timer up in Canada," he says by way of introduction. "Didn't catch the name of it."

The preacher points out that when the Keystone Pioneers performed, they'd often end with "Amazing Grace." He asks them to join him now in singing it.

They do that. It would be better with a fiddle.

The procession to the graveyard is a long one. Aunt Margie counts 36 cars and is sure she missed some.

Past yard sales they drive with their headlights on, past empty bird cages and rows of zinnias and tables full of glassware on the grass. People stand in their yards wondering if they should wave. Shorty's being buried, they know. This is a small town.

Past the borough limits they drive, past Holstein grazing in the ironweed, and once, past an Amish buggy with the horse jingling in its harness and the woman nodding in her bonnet, for she knows, too.

They stand now beside their cars and wait for the grandchildren to lift the casket from the Cadillac. Tripping on the grass mats, they move under the maroon canopy and crowd behind the immediate family seated and clutching their handkerchiefs. Workmen stand a ways off wiping their hands on their jeans.

The preacher says something about being surrounded by the sounds of life, and they hear the cars on the highway and the cicadas in the trees.

They get into their cars and drive back to town. They eat sandwiches and pumpkin pie in the basement of the church. They talk about making ice cream on hot summer days like this one, but when life was simpler. They promise they will visit more often.

"I shouldn't say this," says a nephew from Maine, "But I'm having a good time."

"Shorty would want it that way," his mother says as expected. "Besides, who knows when we'll all be together again?"

He smiles and looks around the room.

"I hope not too soon," she adds.

A Two-Computer Guy

Change, he told them. Take risks. Be bold. Act.

They had come to hear about technology and about learning. And who better to tell them than a top executive of one of the world's most respected corporations?

He stood before them in his shirtsleeves, wiry, animated, and full of fight. Raised in a mill town and educated close to home, he had risen to international stature while half of his fellow employees had lost their jobs.

Change or be left behind, he told his audience, many of them PhDs, and they listened with respect. Celebrate change, he said.

"Endorse it. Embrace it. It doesn't end." They nodded with their fingers on their chins.

Who could argue with the proof pacing before them, tapping at his laptop when he passed it, and the words on the big screen changing behind him?

Americans work hard. That is our heritage. Yet today, I read, we work more hours in a week than ever.

It should come as no surprise, then, that so many showed up on a Saturday morning, no surprise that so many turned off the alarm and stood in the shower and gulped coffee and dressed for the office as if it were any other work day, because for so many, it was.

Oh, we are a busy lot. Yet I cannot help but wonder, what are we busy about? Is it about success? And what is that?

Ah, I could string the interrogation points from here to the end of the column. Most people, I have learned, I will never understand. We keep so much hidden. I can hope to understand only myself. And here I am, contemplating my own navel (if I had one, but that's another story), tapping away in the spare bedroom, writing this as the light leaves the sky and night presses down upon the surface of the lake, working again this evening because I didn't finish over the weekend.

I have two computers, one at the office and one at home. Both are hooked to the Internet. They have made me powerful.

I can send a message to an old friend in Capetown in a nanosecond. I can follow play-by-play for all of Division I football in one steady flow of type. If I wanted to, I could post a picture of my gleaming self and add a bit of original verse for the world to admire.

The possibilities are endless. I can do just about anything, anything but take the time to lie in the grass and watch the swifts swirl above the pines, feeding and twittering in the blue dusk, anything but take the time.

The more I become connected with the world, the less I feel connected to it. The more I sit in front of a screen, the less I stand under the open sky. The more I look at pixels, the less I see.

There is no doubt. Technology has complicated my life. Yes, I can do so much, learn so much, create so much. Yet I feel diminished.

Theodore Roethke talks about that moment when the small drop forms, but does not fall. That is the moment I am missing. I am missing the pure present.

Without the pure present, there can be no reflection. Without reflection, there can be no inner peace.

We need those moments to let our minds wander. Untethered, our thoughts elevate. Sailing, Emerson called it. These are the moments that calm the soul. In a life where every conscious moment is tumultuous, how can our spirits be otherwise?

It can be argued that technology has freed us from the drudgery of providing food and shelter. Yet there is a satisfaction that comes from cutting wood, or planting seed, or patching the roof; there is pleasure in necessity. All else, Thoreau wrote, is folly.

Deep stuff from a guy with two computers. Sorry if I have yet to make a point. No time to think.

The Trick of Quiet

For all the marvels of the age, what I value most is quiet. And like most anything of worth, quiet does not come easily.

By quiet I do not mean silence. I mean the sounds of the natural world only, and the sights as well--no growl of engines, no gnash of machines, no throb of the pulse electronic, no horizons blocked by the hard angles of men.

Living as I do in Upper Turkeyfoot, it is possible for me to know quiet. I walk these fields and woods in search of a peace increasingly rare. Sometimes, I find it. For that, I am thankful.

I seek quiet now as I write this, sitting on the cabin porch, rocking in a weathered Mission rocker, its armrests gnawed by squirrels. Through bare trees to the west, sunlight flows in ribbons of yellow between long, blue clouds.

I see no rooftops, no roads. I see only the line of the wooded hill against the clouds, only the maze of bare twigs and dark, rough trunks rising from the russet mosaic of fallen leaves.

I hear tires on the highway beyond the hill. I hear jets overhead. I hear the revving of a chainsaw and, a moment ago, I heard the ululation of a siren.

In the valley, I hear the blows of a hammer. A dog yelps far away. A gunshot tears through these hills.

No, it is not so quiet this afternoon. But the elements of quiet exist.

A crow complains from hilltop to hilltop. A chickadee arrives at the feeder with a peep and a scratching of its claws. It drops a sunflower seed to the leafmat — we hear it hit — and carries off another with a thrumming of its wings.

A gray squirrel barks in the hollow. The wind rattles leaves clinging still to a young oak.

The dog sighs, her tail thumping on the boards of the porch at the mention of her name. This old rocker creaks.

"I can remember old fellows in my hometown speaking feelingly of an evening spent on the big, empty plains," wrote novelist Sherwood Anderson to a friend.

"It had taken the shrillness out of them. They had learned the trick of quiet."

I have stood alone on the high plains of Wyoming with nothing before me but sky and sage and watched, as the sun set behind me, watched my shadow reach to the unbroken horizon. I know what Anderson meant. That same peace I can find in my own yard, if I try.

The modern world is nothing if not shrill. Too many of us have forgotten the trick of quiet, if we ever knew it.

Too many of us spend every waking moment amid the hum of the workplace or enveloped by the continual chatter of the television. We talk on cellular phones in our cars, as if the radio wasn't intrusion enough. We enter the house and turn on the TV. Automatic.

Our children, when confronted with quiet, I have noticed, grow uneasy, afraid. The absence of distraction to the very young has become as frightening as the absence of light.

Too many of us have lost the ability and the desire to be alone with our own thoughts. Too many of us have lost touch with the natural world that sustains us, and with it our sense of awe.

If we would but seek quiet one hour each day, the world, I believe, would be a saner place.

Jacket Weather: Hooray!

The last thing I need is another coat.

You should see my closet. It's packed. With coats. They're jammed in there under pressure, sardines in can, seeds in a sunflower, scales on a carp, camera crews on the White House lawn — you get the idea.

My wife watches me try to remove one for actual use and shakes her head. It is a struggle; pull too hard and trigger an explosion like a flexed deck of cards, or, more similarly, like opening a tube of dinner roll dough—pow! (I cook sometimes now, and it is frightening, but that's another subject.)

She says I have too many coats

"How many can you wear at a time?" she invariably asks.

"As many as you can pairs of shoes," I invariably reply. I'm bluffing, however, and I hope she never takes inventory.

Before I say more, I admit to a coat fetish. I can't help myself. Being a practical man, I go for function and durability. I like something that looks better with age, material that damage improves, something that sheds rain yet breathes, something just right in cool wind and warm sun, something that would keep me alive for an afternoon on a hilltop in January, something I could wear to the Country Club to unclog a drain.

As you can see, I make many demands on my outerwear. Thoreau said to be blown on by all winds. I am. That is why I need so many coats.

I prefer used stuff, garments that show the wear of shambling humanity — thoroughly disinfected, of course. If I lived in the city, I could walk the streets with my coat cart crying, "New coats for old! New coats for old!"

Instead, I go to thrift stores. Not often, and usually in the next county so as not to embarrass my wife who still runs in the wire wheel with the rest of the corporate gerbils and loves it. That's fine. I support her. She should be so understanding about my coats.

Second-hand stores suit the way I live now, what with my oath of poverty. Neighbors took me along last week.

A retired couple, they live sensibly and frugally. The woman, however, is English and given to whimsy. "The junk shops," as she calls them, satisfy that need. While her husband waits in the van, she shows me the ropes.

We have arrived ten minutes before opening. The building is cement block and windowless. The parking lot is gravel. The excitement is palpable.

Thursday is the best day, she tells me. The Wednesday night volunteers are hard workers, she says, and there's always lots of "new" stuff on display the next morning.

Regulars gather at the door as the time draws near, nodding to each other. A Cadillac sparkles into the lot. It takes all kinds.

As we wait for the manager to remove the padlock and chain from the panic bars, a huge guy in white coveralls jokes, "Feels like I'm back in prison." Everybody chuckles.

The shoppers move in. Experienced bargain hunters cruise the aisles quickly and silently. They have checked out the entire store while I'm still at the coat rack, trying on a rich gabardine topcoat at $10 for the second time, hoping either it somehow grew or I shrunk in the interim. Sadly, no.

Too bad. It would've been just right for getting the mail in a snowstorm.

But I did find a nice cotton sweater for 50 cents. They didn't have change for a twenty, so my neighbor bought it for me.

Her quarters hadn't stopped spinning on the counter before she was out the door. The next junk shop awaited. I didn't find a coat there either, but I did pick up a really nice wig and heart-shaped sunglasses which I wore back to the van. It was a whimsical act, a cheap laugh. You see, I have a bit of English ancestry to which I seldom confess.

Outside, the wind has an edge to it, and the gusts are full of leaves. This is my time of the year: Jacketweather.

I look forward to next Thursday.

Back to Upper Turkeyfoot

We're back, me and the wife and the dogs.

Back to Upper Turkeyfoot. Back to strong wind and bright stars. Back to the old farmhouse where the snow drifts against the kitchen door and the squirrels sleep in the attic.

That's the pleasant part. What pains me is the packing.

The sight of my possessions stacked in a rented truck is a sad thing, the pathetic accumulations of a lifetime contained in a big yellow box. Life as freight—a reminder that the things we care about most cannot be boxed and hoisted, that what matters most is incredibly light.

I'm getting good at this.

At the post office you can find a "Mover's Guide." The cards inside make the change of address official — wouldn't want the taxing bodies to lose track of you.

The guide offers tips like, "eat your canned goods and clean out the refrigerator." No problem there. You should also tell the wife to stop baking pumpkin pies and buying bags of bite-sized powdered sugar donuts. I'm doing my best to keep up, happy that the scales were packed with the towels days ago.

Another tip offered is to set up your bed right away instead of waiting until you're "dog-tired." Again, easily done. I'm determined to do this in one trip, so the mattress will probably be tied to the truck roof where it will be accessible. In fact, the rocking chair may have to be lashed down on top as well. My wife could sit there. We could jostle down the Turnpike like the Clampitts.

But what you really need to know when you're moving is where to find boxes. Boxes are everything.

If you go to Giant Eagle after 10 p.m. and talk sports with the rockers-and-stockers, they'll toss you banana boxes with handholds.

If you pull around behind the State Store and ring the buzzer, the guy with the clip-on tie will open the door and cart you out small, sturdy boxes just right for glassware and books.

If you ingratiate yourself to the local printer (maybe tell him you'll be needing change-of-address cards for all your usurers) he'll surrender a few ream boxes with lids.

Buy rolls of packing tape and a couple of markers, rent yourself a good dolly with working rollers and strong straps, and you're all set. All except for the human. You'll need a human, one with a strong back and no philosophy. That way, you'll get the truck loaded without too much reflection and self-doubt. There'll be plenty of time for that once you settle in again.

Grab that old radio with the coat hanger antenna from the garage, and crank it up on the porch as you lug. Music to move by. Tune in some mindless station that plays "Proud Mary" and "Born to Be Wild" every 15 minutes. Convince yourself you are doing the right thing, rolling down the river, looking for adventure.

Yet, for all of this, I am eager to return. Having lived there for 22 years, I have place wisdom. The house isn't much, but when I sit in the living room under the adzed beams, it's as if I have X-ray vision; I can see into the ceiling, see through the wiring and the plumbing and the rough-cut joists, see up through the bedroom, passing through every layer of flooring and insulation and rafters and tar paper and straight up into the sky where I know the position of Cassiopeia by the season and the time of night.

And I can stand in my yard and know every swale and hummock. I can look to the ridges blue in the distance and name the mountains. I know the farms spread out before me, the Ream Place, the Knepper Place, the Saylor Place. Though we seldom talk, I feel I know the men who work those fields. They are as important in my world as presidents and generals.

I know rain is coming when I hear the train in the valley. I know where the sun will rise through the bare trees and the low path it will trace on the solstice. I know where the snow will drift across the road and where, come spring, the Maypoles will colonize the woods.

In Upper Turkeyfoot, I know where everything belongs. Myself included.

Woodland Architecture

Great architecture has emerged. Maybe you heard about it.

The Guggenheim Museum in Bilbao, Spain, has opened, and the art world is agog.

The work of American architect Frank Gehry, is praised for its aesthetic power. Critics call it entirely new, startlingly beautiful, and also a good place to hang a picture.

The scale, from what I read, is astounding. The atrium, for example, is nearly 200 feet high. And get this, the whole place is sheathed with titanium. Ah, well, it's only money.

The building is said to have cost $100 million, but that sounds too low. Ask a golfer how much he paid for his titanium driver.

Huge effort has been made to avoid the perpendicular. Everything curves and swoops. The whole place looks as if it were cut out with a scroll saw.

Decorating for the holidays, I once placed cute little wax cottages (candles never meant to be lit) on the mantel above the wood stove. By morning, they had the same look.

I think I'd like to visit the Guggenheim in Bilbao, if only to see if I find it as stunning as everybody else. Could be I underestimate its power, but I think I would not.

My architecture in Upper Turkeyfoot is a gable roof and a fieldstone foundation, and it suits me just fine. For great architecture, I go to the woods.

In the woods, the perpendicular is avoided without effort. Here I witness the upward thrust of life, the downward tug of gravity, and the resulting curves and arches of nature. At work, after all, are the forces of spheres.

I feel the need, at October's end, to work. To the shortening days and the cooling earth I respond as do the chipmunks who crash through the fallen leaves, and the squirrels who scrabble over the weathered cabin siding for the seed I scattered on the sill. They stockpile food; I stack firewood.

Their cache of seeds and nuts must give them the same reassurance that cut wood gives me. How I love to look at it stacked on the porch, the richness in texture and color of the fresh-sawn ends of oak and cherry, their history in their growth rings.

As I sweat, I am joined by a frolic of titmice, appearing for the first time this season. Where have they been all summer, I wonder. Their numbers are decreasing, I know from the birdcounts. Has the resident flock vanished, and are these visitors from the northern latitudes come to accompany me through the winter? Welcome, then.

Bold creatures, I have seen them steal hair for their nests from a horse's mane. I sit for a minute to watch their comings and goings, to listen to their claws scrape on the feeder perch. One swoops over my knees and alights on the unraveling arm of my old wicker chair and is gone. But for a moment I looked him in the eye, and I saw there the wild brief gleam of life.

It slows me down. An old wool blanket I wrap around my legs. I wear a moth-eaten sweater I've had for three decades and a tweed cap someone left in an office years ago. I washed it clean and wear it proudly, having learned the joys of found things. Very well, then, I am an eccentric.

But what greater pleasure could even the Bilbao Guggenheim give me than these posts and beams, these knee braces cut from this very hillside and shaped by hand, unpainted, worm-eaten, but one step removed from the trees that envelope me, and, perhaps, if I let my imagination float freely, perhaps still feeling the urge, though fading, to shed their leaves?

The reviews of the new Guggenheim inevitably compare it with nature. "Like the petals of a flower," they say, or "suggests a rose... so full of natural light."

But what more inspiring buttresses than the spreading limbs of the catkined birches? What more rapturous vaulted ceilings than the billowing clouds and the blue sky? What more entrancing light than the dusk?

That the building is wonderful I have no doubt. But for me, there is no greater architecture than the natural world, existing in spite of me, or with my complete reassimilation. That choice is my own.

Travels with Mickey

There's a mouse in my truck. I'm sure of it. When I turned on the blower the other day, I was showered with confetti.

Having a mouse in your truck is part of living in the country. Other parts are bats in the eaves and squirrels in the attic.

I have both of those, too. I also have a lovely collection of insect wings and legs in the shop light, and I really should take out the panel and dump it sometime soon. But first I want to get rid of the mouse.

I figured he'd leave of his own accord. The ride to town would do it, I thought, especially with the heater blasting and the fan on "4."

But no. All that accomplished was to cover my navy blazer with bits of paper and hair that rushed out of the vents in a disgusting blizzard.

The paper, I know, is paper towel chewed from the roll I keep under the seat. The hair I don't want to think about.

"What happened to you?" asked my co-worker when I walked into the office.

She's used to seeing hair on my coat, considering I live with a woman and dogs. But this was a new look. Think of an old lint roller.

"Mouse in the truck," I said from the hall, shaking a goodly portion of nest from my coat.

"A friend had to go to the garage and have her dash disassembled," she said.

"No problem," I said. "The traffic noise will scare him out. I left the window down."

But the next morning, I was speckled again. This time it was so thick in the cab I held my breath.

Maybe the mouse checked out town and decided to ride back to Upper Turkeyfoot. Or maybe he enjoys velocity. I don't know.

The mouse and I have been commuting together for a week. He's got 250 miles under his pelt now, and if he had a bigger brain he would know all the words to the Bonnie Raitt Collection.

Of course, if he had a bigger brain, he'd be maybe building a split level near the corn crib, and I wouldn't have this problem.

I've been opening the window a crack in the hopes he'll stick out his little head like a dog, and I'll just give him a nudge.

I think this happened because I've been too lazy to put the truck in the garage. The nights turn colder. Maybe the warm engine attracted him like it did a cat once. I learned about the cat when I started up, and I don't want to think about that, either.

So, now what? I could spread a little poison on the floor mat, but I don't want him decomposing behind the speedometer. Besides, that's a tough way to go.

I've considered parking next to the feed mill in the south end of town and leaving my door open.

Or maybe I could go to the automatic car wash and ask the guy to stop the chain when those huge brushes are flailing away.

Or maybe I could go to Wal-Mart and buy the Kathy Lee Christmas tape and play it real loud.

Meanwhile, I'm open to suggestions. I'll ask around. Country folk are full of wisdom.

Fewer Friends

Friends grow fewer as we age. It is a natural thing.

They move away, or we do. They disappoint, or we do. They die. It is a natural thing.

We remember a time, years ago, when we worked hard at friendships, when we sought out new acquaintances, searched for common ground — we could never have too many friends. We thought that then.

But we lose the energy. The task of building more friendships over decades seems daunting. And even if we had the will, we lack the time. So we live, and we make promises, and we watch our friends grow fewer. It is a natural thing.

I think of what Thoreau said about friends. Friendship, he wrote, is never secure; it is no more constant a phenomenon than meteors and lightning.

How sad, in the mizzling rain and baring trees, to know him right.

"Most people are about as happy as they make up their minds to be," Abraham Lincoln said. I have it taped to the wall, a page from a calendar promoting salesmanship. Each day has a quote — a year of aphorisms, all aimed toward increasing the bottom line. So. I have come to this, looking to "The Excellence in Customer Service" desktop calendar for inspiration.

Immersed, as I am, in the institutions of man, I tear off the days, one aphorism at a time, until I can explore once more the woods and fields I miss so much. Seeking comfort, I go to a journal of a few years back, notes made in the open air:

• • •

I awoke today with my disappointment, but it doesn't last. Sunlight shatters in the grass, gleams in the pine boughs. Beyond the bright and shining field, rain hangs in bare treetops set ashimmer by the rising wind.

This is no morning for town. No, this morning I shall seek contentment in the fields and woods that surround me, forgetting for a while the relentless, thin suburban present.

This morning I shall seek out that good place only I can provide, for are we not finally the source of our own joy?

I make a few calls, fight off an attack of responsibility, and sit now on a birch log watching oak leaves sail down around me. The forest floor is russet with them.

I peel back the leaf mat, layer by layer, oaks on top, then poplar and cherry, then birch, then maples: always the same order, always cycles. I find comfort in the constancy of nature.

I hear the cheep of chickadees and the bark of a nuthatch. The wind moans in bare branches, finding its winter voice. I go now to the woodland pond, already seeing in my mind the clouds reflected in its onyx surface, the water dark with tannin.

On the way, I find myself clutching to the vestiges of summer: the earthworm stretched upon the rock, the grasshopper green in the shelter of the groundhog hole, the sunlight warm on bare skin.

I am reluctant to let the season go. I regret not having lived it more fully, preoccupied as I have been with the illusory compensatory future.

The present escapes if we let it. Meteors and lightning. Yet at the pond, enclosed in woods and sky, I regain the moment.

Poplar seeds spiral down onto the black water. I see rings expand around them. I smell the decay of leaves. I hear the piping of birds at my back. I feel the air move over me. I taste the moment.

I have found my own good place. I feel myself at the center of my own reality, responsible for my own happiness, while time races away in all directions like rings around a poplar seed. I am content.

Meteors and lightning and friends... The marvel is that they exist at all.

After the Miracle

Leaves fall on us.

We are home and happy. Quality of life returns. It is a blessing.

We sit cross-legged on the aromatic detritus of summer. Leaves rain down through shafts of sunlight; each breeze touches off a bright shower and lets in a little more sky.

In these woods, the suffering of surgery seems far away, in time and distance. A healthy mind holds fast the images of pleasure and lets the others go. That, too, is a blessing.

Yet one scene remains vivid. Perhaps because it captures a delicate balance between life's stages, a thin space between then and now, a brief pause in the flow of living when the truth rises up before you, and you can see, for a moment, into tomorrow.

They are a young couple in their prime. We don't know much about them — Americans, we'd guess, but they could be from anywhere. People from all over the world come to this transplant center seeking miracles.

The husband possesses Teutonic handsomeness; even from his wheelchair he exudes strength, smiling as the nurses stop to wish him well, his discharge papers in his lap.

His wife stands at his side where she has persevered for six weeks. He has received a small bowel transplant. They have four young children.

From our room across the hall we have watched him being carted in and out. We have watched the doctors come and go, sometimes in flocks (this is a teaching hospital), huddling outside the doorway to flip through his chart and mutter amongst themselves before sweeping into his room and speaking in confident tones about the next procedure.

We have watched his wife at the foot of his bed, watched her wither in private moments, then gather herself, muster her hope and her faith and her determination to make it all work. It happens every day on every floor of this hospital. Bravery is commonplace.

They wait now for Transportation, for the workers in the burgundy vests whose job it is to wheel patients from room to room and eventually out the front door and into the street.

The couple wait in the hall by the nurses' station. Caretakers and decision-makers flow around them like a stream around a stone. The good-byes and good-lucks have stopped. One can only say so much.

They wait to go home. Every day for six weeks they have waited to go home. And as they wait, the final minutes before their release grow enormous. Time is elastic.

He tires. His pain shows. He slouches in his chair, though still managing a smile for passersby. Behind him, his wife touches her forehead, sweeping back a lock of dark hair. Her rings sparkle, her fingers tremble. She is exhausted. They wilt before our eyes.

I leave my wife's bedside and step into the hall to say something. It will be all right, I say. It has to be.

They nod. He stares at his hands on his papers on his lap. She looks me in the eye and thanks me without a word. Her fear has passed. In her gaze I find only acceptance. So this is how it is. She has seen tomorrow.

Too soon, I think. Too soon are they ejected into the current of every day life, where the smallest thing, buying groceries for example, can sweep them away.

But that's the way it is now. That is the system. Costs, you understand.

Leaves fall on us.

We watch them fall among the tall dark trunks; the oaks stem first in a slow spin, some floating as stable as the hulls of ships; the sugars wagging saffron; the birches in tight spirals; the cherry in barrel rolls, the poplar in long dips, escalloped like the flight of a woodpecker.

We hear them crash into the deepening, magnificent litter. We pick up a handful, crush them, and hold them to our nose, grateful.

Leaves of Bent Grass

EDITOR'S NOTE: *O'Brien found himself one warm afternoon in late October torn between his art and his golf. In a flash of what he insists was genius, he slipped a book, a pen, a notebook, and binoculars into his bag and hit the open links. What follows is a work of nine stanzas. He claims he played with Walt Whitman.*

Prologue
I celebrate golf, and sing golf, and what I assume you shall assume, for you weren't there so you'll have to take my word for it. Besides, poets deal in truth.

I
Loaf with me on the first tee, camerada, loose the cover from your driver.

Not words, nor music, nor strategically timed clearing of throats do I want, only the lull I like, only the wind at my back, only the pure tink of titanium, the somersaulting tee, the soaring ball rising into the vaults of heaven, the "You da' man!"

Dazzling, tremendous nine iron flying right. You villain wedge! You vagrant fluffer of effete chips!

Two putts for bogey, but am I not alive?

II
The spotted hawk swoops by and accuses me, he complains of my gab and my practice swings. I, too, am not a bit tamed, having bladed a four iron.

But the ball sails low under the moaning gibberish of dry limbs, careens off the bank and trickles onto the green.

The birdie putt dies with half the ball over the lip. When the ball hangs but does not fall, that is the pure present. Tap in for par.

III
I am large. I contain multitudes. I need them on this long par five. I shape my drive around the pines, and the ball comes to rest in the middle of the sprawling sward, the scenery plain in all directions.

A comrade lives along this fairway. His wife, the essence of womanhood, has erected corn shocks and set out pumpkins to mark their yard as out of bounds.

Toward the distant hills I fling my fancies, and nearly my three iron as well, after a thin hit has left me at the bottom of the hill still 100 yards from the pin.

I prepare my being, I immerse my soul. Elbow in, head still, follow through. Three putts for bogey. I make notes on the sufferings of man, and as I scribble, my pull cart drifts unnoticed down the slope and upsets. I sound my barbaric yawp over the roofs of the summer homes.

IV

Ever the silent, splendid sun. Ever the straight drive and the true iron, the pin-high chip and the hollow rattle of the dropping putt.

I sing the body electric. Sweet mother earth provides. In the deep rough on the way to the next tee, I find a new Titleist.

V

The course is quiet. Only the bark of chipmunks, the scream of jays, the twitter of a bat feasting on the insects floating in crepuscular light.

My drive tops the hill from where the purple stacks of the Alleghenies spread out before me. Possessed by the spirits of all who have eagled this hole before me, I launch a sweet four iron over the trees to the edge of the green.

A smooth chip sends the ball curling toward the pin. I am an acme of things accomplished, an encloser of things to be. The ball rolls over the hole and off the back.

A chip long, a putt short, a bogey. On the cart path, a brass plaque on a boulder reads, "In Memory of Les Basinger." I wonder if Number Five figured in Les' demise. But as to you Death, and your bitter hug of mortality, it is idle to try to alarm me.

VI

I cross the road, the toughest holes ahead of me, and I think of the turbid pool that lies in the autumn forest, the black stems that decay in the muck, along with a couple a hundred TopFlites.

But today I fling my likeness after the rest and true as any on the shadow'd wilds.

I clear the lake. I pick up just 130 yards from the pin because The Pro is topdressing the green, and the way I'm hitting them, I'd kill him sure. I award myself a bogey.

VII

Ever the towering eight iron and the short putt. Par.

VIII

Ever the glorious drive down the middle and the soulful thunk of a six iron sticking in the soft green. Par.

IX

Ever the high cut over the sussurrous oaks and the six-footer that falls in the side door. Par.

I ring the big bell as I pass it on this last, blind fairway, not because there is anyone behind me, but because I want to hear it echo across the continent. I hear it still.

I depart as air, I shake my white Callaway cap at the runaway sun, I effuse my flesh in eddies, and drift it in lacy jags. I read Whitman, I wrote a column, and I shot 40. Allons!

Attending to November

I had a good day today. I stayed home.

It's been a while since I spent the day at home in Upper Turkeyfoot, the whole day. I have seen too much of offices these last few weeks, attended too many meetings, completed too many projects.

Now, I like my office in town. It has windows facing west, and I can watch the sun set behind rooftops and steeples through the blind slats.

Working late, alone with my computer, I feel the bass notes from the band in the bar across the street, feel them thumping in the concrete and the steel and in my very bones. I know when it is closing time, for I can hear the car doors slam and the engines start unmuffled amid the shouts of profane young men.

Driving home through the pale hills under the cusp of a moon and a few brilliant stars--it is one of those cool, still nights when smoke bends out of chimneys and hangs in the treetops in flat, unbroken bands — driving home, noting how exhaustion sensitizes me, I decide I have had enough of town.

So today I stayed home, spent it working under the sky, getting the feel of November, attending to the business of the season.

Today I replaced the furnace filters and swept out the cellar. My basement is wet, and this pleases me.

These old farmhouses often were built over a spring. In the yard, my well is hand-dug and lined with fieldstone. Remove the concrete cap, and you would see it is the width of a man's shoulders.

This old frame house is here because of the presence of water and the absence of wind, built in an age, not so long ago, when man , as he chose a place to live, considered the elements instead of the amenities, when he was more attuned to nature.

This well for generations has supplied both humans and livestock. The water table is high here below the hilltop. My cellar will never be dry. It would be useless to try and seal the water out; better only to direct its path. Besides, I like the salamanders in my basement. Old timers will tell you salamanders are a sign of good water.

So I stay home. Today I climbed through the trapdoor to the roof and sealed the flashing with asphalt. Down the chimneys I peered and was pleased to find little creosote. Old timers tell me they used to lower into the chimney a live goose, and its flapping cleaned the flue. But I don't know if I believe it. Old timers love a story.

Today I sat on the roof ridge for a while. The woods are open now, reduced by oak leaves falling and blackbirds rising, leaving the trees bare save for the nests of squirrels and crows. From here I can see into Maryland. From here the wind is stronger, the sky wider.

Today I glazed storm windows and raked walnuts, staining my hands with their softening husks. Today I swept the porch and washed windows, my fingers cold and stinging.

Today I stacked wood, and repaired a dripping faucet, and cut a young ash for a clothes prop.

Today I delighted in simple tasks. Today I received more enjoyment from fixing the keeper on the stable door than from all the business of the office.

Today I watched an angle of geese pass over. Today a few snowflakes fell. Today I lit a fire.

I go to bed tired and content and filled with a sense of accomplishment. How little it takes to make us happy.

Old Apples

Steam roils off the logshed roof as the sun rises, and frost recedes into the woods. A junco feeds beneath the pine— the snowbirds are arriving.

Through deep clover we wade to the edge of the woods and sit beneath the apple tree on the hilltop. We feel this old earth spin.

Most leaves are down, all save the oaks, and we hear the wind in them. We watch them move, russet and ocher. We watch them fall.

A chickadee sings its April song. Pee-vee, it sings. In some ways, we witness a second spring. Buds have formed on birch saplings. Fiddleheads are rolled up tight in their husks. In the woods, we hear calls unfamiliar, the notes of transients changing continents.

We sit under this old apple tree and look through the bright autumn air, so clear we can make out the crowns of individual trees on the ridge across the valley.

The woods has become a sunny place, and the treetops fill with sky. Somewhere in the bleaching stalks of timothy we hear a cricket, a single cricket, and we try to absorb its song, to store it in our cells that we might hear it, as well, in January.

Under this old tree we sit, the woods at our back, looking down across the field toward the old farmhouse. The apples hang gleaming and pendulous in the cold wind.

Late to ripen, big, and tart, I believe them to be Northern Spy, one of the old varieties. Some lie in the curling leaves among the fading asters, and the deer have made a path to them. Hear the crunch as we bite in, feel the juices flow!

The old apples are disappearing, replaced by hybrids you can pick without a ladder and eat without delight. This old tree, nearly two feet across, is the last remnant of an orchard that once covered this field.

One other survivor used to drop its sweet, yellow fruit near the road — a Pound Sweet, I think. The cat bore her young in its hollow trunk before a heavy snow broke it off at the ground.

A neighbor who still tends his family's cranberry bog gave me a catalog that features antique apples. I've spent hours reading it.

There are Spitzenburgs, favored by Thomas Jefferson. There are Yellow Newtown Pippins, bred by the colonists to keep well on the voyage back to England. There are Maiden's Blushes and Rambos and Russets. There are Tompkins Country King, considered by many the best out-of-hand apple ever.

Just this week I heard the name of the man who built that old two-story house framed now in the arms of this tree. John Marker cleared these fields with oxen before he left to fight for the Union. I like to think he planted this apple tree whose fruit we eat and in whose dappled shade we sit.

John Marker is buried, I am told, in a back corner of the Methodist cemetery in the village. I shall look for his grave. Perhaps I'll leave an apple there, one of these.

The World We Look For

Do me a favor. Slow down.

Life was meant to be lived slowly. Of that I am convinced. Job, family, institution, society — all conspire toward a quicker pace. It is difficult to resist. Later, we think, later we will relax. But there is never a later.

Slowly. I am convinced. Live slowly.

I want you to take just a half an hour a week, just 30 minutes, and do nothing.

All I'm asking is that you devote half an hour to sit under the open sky in solitude.

Just sit. Just for 30 minutes. That's the length of a sitcom. I hereby propose a new unit of time. Let us call it a "Seinfeld."

All I ask is that you devote a Seinfeld a week to contemplation in the open air.

Never before have such large masses of people been so totally divorced from the land, so alienated from nature.

It astonishes me how many people have never seen the Milky Way. They have never been without artificial light.

I also find it surprising that so few of us are aware of the present phase of the moon. At what are we looking?

So, find a spot you like. It need not be far away. Find a place that pleases you, but make it be outside. Seek quiet.

Living as I do in Upper Turkeyfoot, it is possible for me to know quiet. I walk the fields and woods in search of a peace increasingly rare. Sometimes, I find it. For that, I am thankful.

But I realize that finding a quiet place may be more difficult for you. So let it be enough if your place contains the elements of quiet, a place where, at the very least, you can hear the wind. Most importantly, it must be a place where you will not be interrupted as you do nothing, a place where you can be alone with your own thoughts.

I'm not asking much — a Seinfeld a week. All you have to do is nothing. Just sit. Be still. Dress warmly, in layers. Wear wool, maybe something to break the wind and shed the rain.

Annie Dillard, raised in Pittsburgh, while a writing student at Hollins College in Roanoke, found such a spot along a small stream that ran through the campus.

"Beauty is real," she writes in Pilgrim at Tinker Creek. "The appalling thing is that I forget it."

Watching the water one November afternoon, she was startled by three migrating Canada geese that "thundered across the pond." As is usual with geese, she heard them before she saw them, yet they flew so close she "felt the flayed air slap at (her) face."

"It is the shock I remember," she says.

"Not only does something come if you wait," Dillard writes, " but it pours over you like a waterfall, like a tidal wave. You wait in all naturalness without expectation or hope, emptied, translucent, and that which comes rocks and topples you; it will shear, loose, launch, winnow, grind. . .

"This distant silver November sky, these sere branches of trees, shed and bearing their pure and secret colors — this is the real world."

So I ask you to pick your spot and sit. Just sit. It happens on its own. A door opens for you where you never knew a door existed. It does if you let it.

Sitting is a colder occupation than walking. Don't let the weather stop you. Wool does the trick.

Do this for yourself. Find your spot. Sit. Nature won't disappoint you, given the chance. Go simply, without expectation.

Caught up in America, we have forgotten how much is enough. We have been tricked into believing we will find happiness in more.

It is possible to have more by wanting less. Thoreau was right about that.

What can you expect? An epiphany? It is possible. It is possible, if you are warm and comfortable and undisturbed. Being still, you see deeper. Nature, like art, requires the long look.

So go to your spot in the dawn and go in the dusk. Go in the sun and in the rain and in the biting cold. Go, and do nothing. The world will reveal itself by degrees. Contentment is easily found, once we stop seeking it.

"Having found this one place," Thoreau said, " I now find it in another...So, in the largest sense we find only the world we look for."

May you find the world you look for. May it find you.

Not Sold in Stores

Wood smoke curls out of chimneys in Upper Turkeyfoot. It rises white in moonlight through the leafless trees.

In the morning, we find ice in the dogs' water bucket. The first snow has come and gone, flattening the stalks of timothy in the field, compressing the leaf mat in the woods. Shovels stand ready on porches. Snowtreads are mounted on pickups.

It seems as if winter never left these old mountains, as if it lay hidden in the earth and rises now.

Afternoons may warm, the sun may burn our cheeks, but winter is here, sure enough; we feel it through the soles of our boots. We wear wool.

This, for me, is the season of nostalgia. In brown November, I think of my great-grandfather. Permit me this indulgence.

His house stood above an old mill race in the village of Neshannock Falls, a community defined by the creek that ran through it. The structure is still there, but it has been remodeled; the springhouse is gone, and the trains no longer run through the trees behind the house. You see why I use the past tense?

In summer my great-grandfather sat in the yard and watched my brother and me run through the orchard and whip apples at each other with sharpened sticks. He sat in his suspenders, his blue workshirt buttoned to the neck, and he rocked under the giant oak. His father, a veteran of Gettysburg, had died on that very spot.

I used to stand on the back rungs of his rocker and give him a ride. I broke one once. He never raised his voice.

In winter he sat before the fireplace. I remember the sounds — the popping of the fire, the ticking of the clock on the mantle, the voices of my grandmother and her sisters and their daughters performing miracles in the kitchen around the bulging, black cookstove.

No television. No radio. No intrusions of a rude world. Only the sounds of family, of fire, of time.

And sometimes, too, the sound of my great-grandfather's wrath. The mention of Harry Truman would set him off. He never forgave him for firing MacArthur, this son of a soldier for Lincoln.

I remember the pitcher pump at the kitchen sink, the trap door to the root cellar, the cold walk to the outhouse.

I remember firelight lambent on his creased face and on his gnarled hands. That is mostly what I could see with the cold dark on my back and the long shadows of the andirons expanding into the room — the hands and faces of family in firelight, smiling at each other, accepting this old man's cussing with little more than a tisk.

I remember leaving, stepping outside to the sound of rushing water, to the sweet smell of apples rotting on the ground. I remember the rumble of planks in the covered bridge and the drive through the night to our house and its garish, electric brightness.

A reader called this week to ask what has happened to Thanksgiving. She wants to decorate her home with Pilgrims and turkeys, and can find none. We now move, she noted, directly from Halloween to Christmas.

"Ah, well," she sighed, answering her own question. "I suppose there's no money in it, not much to sell for Thanksgiving."

No, we will not find Thanksgiving in the market place. We should look, instead, in our hearts.

This is a corny sentiment, I know. It seems to me we could use a little more of that.

View from the Cabin

Hope.

I start with that, writing it at the top of the page. It seems an act of defiance.

To think well of our world near the end of the Millennium is to stand against the prophets of doom, to defy the odds, to fly in the face of compounding data on ice caps, ocean currents, deforestation, the accelerating extinction of species, pollution, avarice, mutating bacteria, desertification, and — most frightening of all — our own numbers.

So many of us. So many of us.

To write "hope" and mean it seems the pronouncement of the ignorant or the innocent. I am neither, yet I write it.

Hope.

It seems the giggle of an idiot. Very well, then, I am simple-minded. I write it again.

Hope.

I can write it and mean it because of where I am at this moment. I write this in longhand, disdaining even the manual typewriter on its swing-out shelf under this wide maple desk in the cabin in the woods. Mice have nested in the old Royal again I see, the springs and levers packed with shredded tissue and newsprint.

Writing with pen and paper slows me down, thoughts form into clauses, clauses into sentences. A machine, you see, gets into the writing; the pen is best suited to the flow of reason. The mice can stay where they are for now.

Where I am gives me hope. I write in a circle of light from an oil lamp. A fire warms my back. This cabin I built by hand, without power tools. The boards and posts were sawn from logs cut from these hills and salvaged from a closed sawmill. The siding is chestnut stripped during the renovation of a barn in the next township, the wood creased and veined by weather.

I write surrounded by woods, branches bent and glazed with ice, every tip of leaf and twig bangled. I hear the fire guttering and the melt dripping off the roof as steady as a metronome. My back is warm, my knees cold under the desk.

In such a place I have the luxury of simple-mindedness. I am content to feed the fire (a welcome break from translating sensations into words).

I am content to sit all day and watch the ice thicken and the branches bend and the birds come and go for the sunflower seed and cracked corn I scatter.

Spending the day here in this 12-by-18 foot room, beyond the reach of society, beyond the news, clears the head and opens the heart. Such surroundings heighten a reverence for all things, for the basic elements of fire and air, earth and water. It is, I think, a Hindu saying that God sleeps in stones, lives in plants, moves in animals, and creates in man. That seems about right in these icy woods with the light fading.

Each wall has a window, each a tall, double-paned panel from a set of sliding patio doors discarded by a friend. They reach from floor to ceiling, from ground to sky, except for one placed horizontally above the desk where I sit. Looking out across the wooded hollow I watch the shape of the next hill grow faint as the freezing mist falls and the ice thickens.

The sill above the desk is filled with found things: birds nests and feathers, oak galls and snail shells, gnawed hickory nuts (each squirrel chews a distinctive opening, and you can tell by the hole if it was a red, a gray or a flying squirrel), the skull and beak of a crow, the antlers of a buck, the broken eggshell of a grouse, a stone with a fossil--all found things, all rich in the elements of life, all offering hope.

The room is spartan: bare wood, a bed, a stove, an ash bucket, a place to sit, a desk. On the desk I write in my oval of yellow light. Three books stand at the corner--Emerson's Essays, Whitman's Leaves of Grass, and Thoreaus' Walden, all old, their spines darkened by readers' palms--books just right for freezing mist and firelight.

A simple life is still possible, if we work at it, if we sacrifice, if we come to understand that less is more. That is my hope.

You may have read this far and remain pessimistic. But a book or a newspaper column can only be, at best, charts to sail by. You must have an original experience with the natural world if you are to lose your nihilism. I cannot bring the gifts of nature to your table. Nature is real only when you reach out and touch it with your hands.

Naturalist John Burroughs with his long white beard once told a group of school children in New York City, "With me, the secret of youth in age is the simple life — simple food, sound sleep, the open air, daily work, kind thoughts, love of nature, and joy and contentment in the world in which we live."

He said that in 1911. It remains sound advice, and today assumes a sense of urgency. Today, optimism may be the ultimate form of rebellion.

May I end as I began. That is my wish.

Hope.

Winter

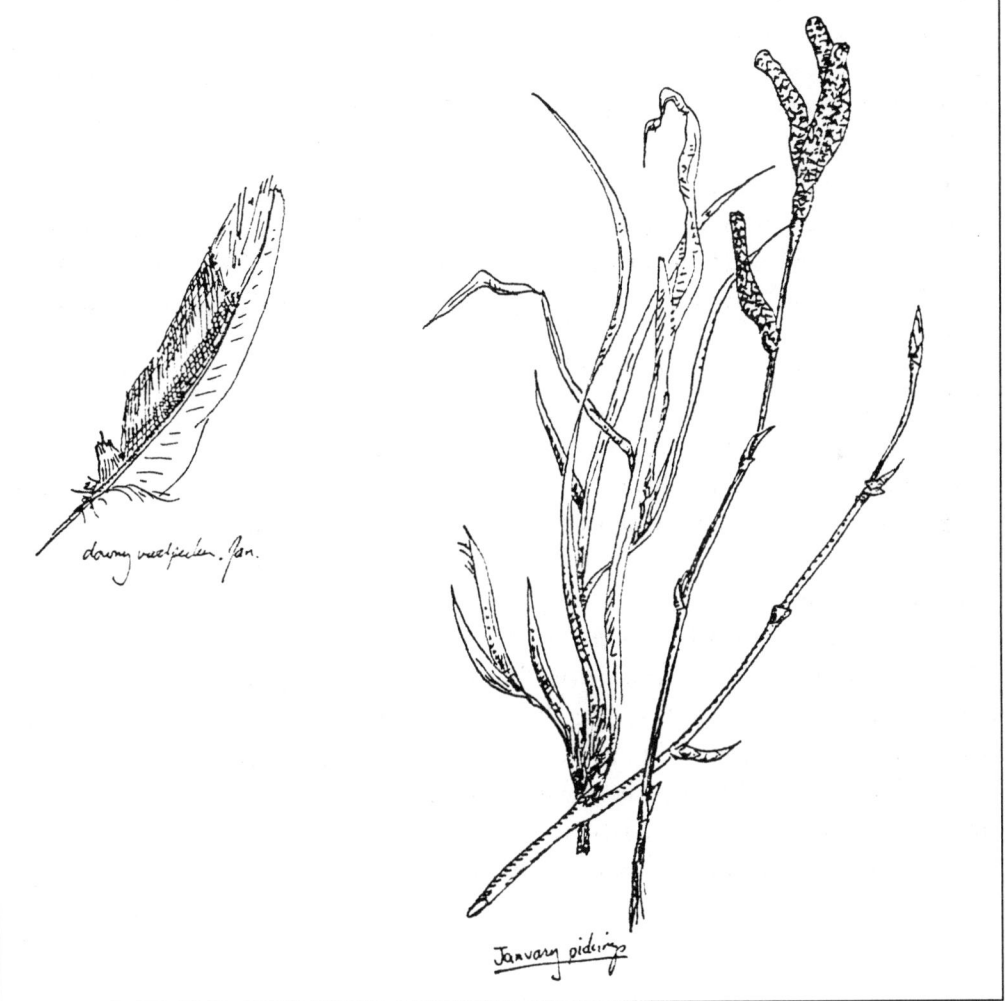

November Boarders

"I hear something," she said.

No response.

"A noise. I hear a noise," she said again, this time succeeding in awakening me. I heard it, too.

"It's nothing," I said. "Old houses have noises." I closed my eyes.

And they do. Timbers creak in strong storms. Tossing pine boughs sometimes scrape against the panes. Winter wind sometimes finds its way through these old window frames and sets the zinc tracks buzzing like kazoos.

But this was the noise of a live thing — a mouse gnawing, I figured. Yet I kept my suspicion to myself. I am more tolerant of a mouse than is my wife.

A mouse in the house is routine for November in Upper Turkeyfoot. I don't mind them; they are considerate boarders, all things considered. They are cleaner than, say, a dog, and certainly less demanding. They are more peaceable than, say, a serial-killer cat crouching in the shrubbery under the bird feeder.

Mice make no demands. I accept them. In fact, I might not even know they have moved in except for the occasional scamper across the suspended ceiling in the kitchen when I come down stairs and flick on the light to join my little friends in a midnight snack.

Another way I know is when my wife awakens me in the middle of the night.

Outside, many of the creatures that stay the winter have hunkered down. The gray squirrels have pulled together massive nests of leaves and grapevine bark high in the oaks. The groundhogs have moved from their summer burrows in the field to their winter chambers in the sheltering woods.

The opossums and the muskrats and the garter snakes and the skunks and the bats and the bears are going to sleep. The frogs and the turtles and the tadpoles lie dreaming in muck. At least I like to think that they dream, perhaps of warmer days, as we do.

In November in the country you expect visitors. They check in for the winter. Red Squirrels make a nest of carpet padding in the attic. Moles grope their way through the fieldstone foundation to spend the harsher months in the cellar. For moles, it must be like moving to the Keys.

The chipmunks are content to doze in their dark chambers under the lilac bush. But the red squirrels like buildings. Already they have stashed this year's bumper crop of black walnuts in every conceivable nook and cranny of the barn, the log shed, and the garage. If I don't start the pickup for a few days, I have to open the hood and toss out the green husks, as big and round as baseballs, lest they foul the fanbelt. I throw them into the field, where I hope they will sprout.

Last winter the squirrels cavorted every sunny morning in the attic. This fall, I tied a line around my chest, climbed out the trapdoor and onto the roof, hung over the edge, and clogged their entranceway with expanding foam. It looks awful, like maybe an emu had perched there for days. But I accomplished my mission: mornings are quieter, and I didn't die.

So, a mouse — no problem.

"There it is again," she said, eyes wide. "Please check."

I snapped on the reading light and looked into the wastebasket. A silky little guy with twitching whiskers looked me in the eye. His pink feet gripped the edge of an empty box of Wheat Thins — empty to me, maybe, but provender to him. I turned off the light.

"A mouse," I said.

"A mouse!" she said.

"He'll run up the chimney and into the attic," I said. But no. He chomped away.

"Please," she said, pathetically.

I covered the top of the wastebasket with Volume II of Thoreau's journals, carried the whole works downstairs into the kitchen, and went back to bed. Henry wouldn't mind, I was sure. In the morning, I turned him loose in the yard. Maintaining biodiversity and matrimonial harmony requires diplomacy and compromise. Next time I empty a box of crackers, I'll lift a panel and put it above the kitchen ceiling. I trust you not to mention it.

No Ugly Days

The weatherman, I'm thinking, is wrong.

It's not his forecast that has me shaking my head. As for temperature and precip' ("bundle up and take along that umbrella,") he's most likely right. At his command, after all, is the Super Jumbo Doppler Storm Tracker 2,000. Every time he mentions it, I'm impressed.

Plus, he went to school for this, which is probably where he first learned to say "bundle up and take along that umbrella."

But, no, it's not his forecast. It's his opinion of today that puzzles me.

"An ugly, ugly day out there," he says. This leaves me wondering just how much time he spends "out there."

"Foggy, drizzly, chilly — just plain ugly," he says shuddering in gabardine. "A good day to stay inside."

My advice would be just the opposite. In Upper Turkeyfoot, there is no such thing as an ugly day. Not when you're actually "out there."

A weatherman, you'd think, would appreciate all weather. True, in the extreme, the elements can scare the isobars out of you. Remember the thrills in "Twister."

But today is far from extreme. Today is what the Irish call "soft" weather. I call it beautiful. I have learned to enjoy the low key, and it takes considerably less to thrill me than a cow flying across my windshield.

Let me tell you about it:

The rain intensified with the dawn. The seasons, as always are a series of advances and retreats, the winter gaining by degrees. Ice grows in shards on the pond in the clear, spangled night, only to melt under the clouds and the warm rain of the next afternoon. Advance and retreat.

At last a sort of equilibrium is reached, and we have a few days when the mercury barely moves, and the clouds hang low and motionless as if caught upon the hills. This is such a day.

On such a day, you will not see your neighbor about, unless he be orange and armed. But you will see crows. I saw them this morning flying in the fog, dark and indistinct, stretched out single file, each one yelling as it passed over me. I took it as a greeting.

Their even spacing intrigues me. Could it be they fly at the limit of visibility (500 yards today, I'd guess)? The weatherman would know that if he had at his command a device as sophisticated and reliable as a family of crows.

They live as tribes, brothers and sisters, aunts and uncles, cousins and grandparents, surviving as a unit, smart enough to avoid man, overseers of these ridges and valleys, sentinels for all that lives here, or rather, for all that listens.

Yesterday, during a break in the cloud cover when the sun shone for a few minutes, the crows took wing and poured as a mob into the valley, banking and diving, cavorting and calling. I am convinced they did it for the pure joy of the moment, for no other reason than for fun.

Today the weather is far from extreme, yet I find it thrilling still. The beauty of these woods and fields is inexhaustible. The rain and the fog only add to it.

"Even a man waiting to die," writes S.L.A. Marshall in his account of Vietnam, "will notice the loveliness of the trees and the sunlight around him."

What I notice today is the buffed quality of the morning, like worn silver, tarnished and dark in the recesses, the knobs and tumescences rubbed to a soft luster. Rain polishes the day. The dirt road shines with it, as do the brown leaves on the ground, as do the backs of my hands.

"The height of wisdom is to see the miraculous in the common," Emerson said. I am no wiseman, but the common pleases me. I give myself to the near at hand and am content.

I do not need the astonishing, the exciting, the far away. I watch the crows pass over in the mist. I see the rain in pendants on the birch buds. Already, an advance. I wouldn't call it ugly.

What Martha Won't Tell

Country living puts you in touch with nature. Everybody knows that. Even city folk.

Close to the earth, you become attuned to the great systems of the universe: the cycle of life and death, the passing of the seasons, the digestive tracts of animals.

We often discuss here the first two of these wonders, high-minded as we are. But the last one is an element of rural life seldom mentioned. I've never seen it addressed in Country Living, and to my knowledge Martha Stewart has yet to invent a decorative use for dung. But when you live in the country in the company of beasts, dealing with excreta is unavoidable.

This is especially true on warm winter days. The snow melts, the ground uncovers, and there you have it, the accumulations of the season.

We had such a day last week. Bright and balmy broke the morning, a warm breeze blowing out of the south. I grabbed the shovel I keep on the back porch for such occasions and went to work, scouring the yard for coproliths.

I have developed over the years an effective technique I call the Scoop and Sling. With a single pass of the blade I can pick the grass clean and launch the doo-doo through the bright air and into the nearest flower bed. Both my dogs and pansies thrive.

Deep snow is to blame. The dogs, fundamentally tidy creatures, prefer the privacy of the tall weeds in the field. The yard they reserve for decaying groundhogs and the eviscera of "harvested" deer.

But in deep snow they wade only a few feet from the paths, hunkering there with expressions of disgust. And when the thaw comes and I grab my shovel, they lie in the sunshine, blinking and detached, feigning innocence, as if they had no idea.

There are more enjoyable ways to spend a springlike afternoon, to be sure. But scooping and slinging is a priority. Fail to take advantage of a break in the weather and suffer the consequences.

Your boot treads will clog. You will spend hours each week balancing on one leg while you scrape with a stick. Crank up the heater in the truck and be forced to crack a window. In town, sales clerks will shun you, whispering behind your back.

The farmer, too, is thus engaged on such a day. His scooping and slinging is mechanized. With more than a hundred cows, he deals in bulk, cleaning out his barn with a highlift and pulling the spreader over the corn stubble.

You can follow his splattered trail down the paved road to the fields. Breath deep the aroma of the thaw. (Many country people, me among them, claim to like this smell, having no choice.)

We wave to each other as he passes, him in the enclosed cab of his tractor, me with my shovel, country folk. I cover my head with my arm as if to shield myself from the ensuing brown shower. I see him laughing. If I adopt any more dogs, I might ask to borrow his equipment.

Through the yard I walk, full of the satisfaction of a job well done. Slip. Damn.

A neighbor calls from up the road. He's an early riser, and by this time on a Saturday he has usually been to town and back, put away the groceries, and started dinner. Not today.

"Cleaning up the yard," he says when I ask. My neighbor has dogs, too. "Three buckets full already."

I suggest come spring that he dig a few more flower beds within slinging distance.

My neighbor says he hears another Alberta clipper is on its way. Six inches by midnight.

This makes us both happy.

In Deep

I awoke to the thrill of deep snow, the world transformed.

I had hoped for as much, checking the storm's progress in the dark, flipping on the spotlight to see the powder gust and swirl.

Sleep and reading stitched the night together, and it pleased me to watch the well capstone sink into the drift.

In the morning when I raised the blind, brilliance filled the room, a gift.

Deep snow means tending to the near. Such days are whole, complete, as round as pearls.

The birds have gathered in the birch bent to the ground by last week's ice. My appearance with scoop in hand excites them. They would pluck seed from the top of my cap if I stood still long enough and limited their options. But there is work to be done.

I clear the porch. The dog attacks the shovel with each scrape, amusing us both — a Skye terrier, he is low and sturdy and relentless. I open paths — to the barn, to the woodshed, to the mailbox, to the garage. My timing is perfect. A neighbor shows up on his tractor and, with two passes of his backblade, grades my driveway without disturbing the gravel. He swings open the cab door and grins.

"A job well done," I say, leaning on my shovel. We are happy men with nowhere to go but home, for the road is full of snow, great waist-high peaks diagonal from bank to bank, waves cresting.

Nowhere to go. We are in deep, and I prefer it. The township plow will be by soon enough. Tomorrow would be fine.

Today I will glory in the close at hand. Today I will deal with primary concerns, with warmth and shelter and food, for the soul as well as the stomach.

In deep, I will tend the fire and walk the woods. Returning, I will hold steaming tea in both hands, an old book open on the pine table. I will sit in a soft chair under the down quilt. The chair is wide enough for two, going nowhere.

Through the drifts I wade into the field. The weeds above the snow always stun me with their precision, every point and twist and effloresence distinct and sharp and astonishing. I am easily amazed, in deep.

The earth slopes away from me, undulating and unbroken as far as I can see into the valley. I count myself among the privileged poor.

I say that because I hear a new aristocracy rises in our country, a growing class of the rich and powerful, a venal elite.

In New York City, for example, I read the climate is "get rich or get out." I am happy not to be in New York City. I offer one example:

The editor of Vogue gave a party for her food writer. "Naturally," The New Yorker says, "the canapes were excellent." Care for roasted new potatoes topped with white truffles, or perhaps sunny-side-up quail's eggs topped with caviar on lightly sauteed brioche? You wouldn't want to miss thin slices of lardo di maile di Colonnata, thought to be "Michelangelo's favorite pig fat."

(In the room the women come and go, rifting like Michelangelo — with apologies to T.S. Eliot.)

And get this. The hostess hated the carpet, so she called her high society florist who shipped in leaves from New Jersey and scattered them about. "Beautiful, colorful leaves, no browns, but warm tones and with moisture as if they had just fallen."

Smashing. The guests nearly swooned to be eating pig fat with their shoes in real leaves. No one will divulge the cost. Which of us is out of touch?

Plowing ahead through the field toward the woods, I wonder what this deep snow might be worth. Priceless, I'd say.

I stop to examine a hole from which a deermouse has ventured, hopping a foot or so on the surface, thinking better of it, retracing its tracks, and resubmerging. I examine it quickly before the dog torpedoes into the snow with just his circling tail exposed.

I stand and look across the valley as it fills again with falling snow headed our way, obscuring the far hills. In deep, we are lords of all we survey, the dog and me. That seems nobility enough.

Mountain Return

The old house creaks. Snow hits the panes, tiny explosions in the pressing darkness. I fall asleep with the wood stove ticking. Crows wake me. I know I'm home.

I should not have left. I should not have surrendered the peace these woods and fields provide me. A man of my age and experience, I should have known better.

Last summer in this space I had written, "I think sometimes of going home. And would I dream then of these misted, tossing horizons, and of the sunset pink on the bellies of the clouds that stream over these mountains and me? Ah, the soul aches, but for what? Know that, and you have wisdom."

And so I did go, back to the more gentle slopes of my youth, back to the slow creeks and verdant marshes. But it was no longer home. And so I did dream.

I have returned to Upper Turkeyfoot. It is good to be home. Am I the wiser for the upheaval? Has the turmoil clarified the spirit? I can only say perhaps. The longer I live, the more I can only say perhaps.

Perhaps I am a little wiser now. But at a price. When you leave, the space you vacate closes in behind you.

I had chickens once. In the coop they had their own society, and I admired them for it. If a hen were to escape and strut freely about the yard for one glorious afternoon of scratching and feasting, the pecking order would quickly adjust to her loss. Snag her by the leg with a wire hook, return her flapping and squawking to the coop, and she would be immediately attacked. Mostly, they survived it. I do not now admire the society of chickens as much as I once did.

So, yes, I sacrificed much to leave, and more, I think, to return. Sometimes, I have learned, it is better to wonder "what if?" than to know.

But as I unpack boxes in the cold and echoing kitchen, as I put things back where they belong, I see nuthatches hopping down the pine bark toward the feeder. Cardinals arrive. Juncos hop about in the sopping snow.

The window above the sink frames the hilltop against the pewter sky. It is a form I know better than my own face.

I love the rows of hay stubble curving up the slope. I love the yard with its islands of grass rising from the melting snow. I love the crow awakening me.

On the sill, in an old bottle I had found below the sugar camp, the flowers I had picked last visit have withered and dried. The asters are bearded with seed, parachutes ready for the wind. I open the door and release them. I have catching up to do.

I am home, where I can wear my goofy cap with ear flaps; home, where I can hear the crows; home, where I know quiet has a sound.

I tie the dog on the porch. He vanishes into his house and sticks his nose out from under the rug that covers the hole, just his nose. His tail thumps against the side.

Over the snow crust I walk, the stars over and around me, the constellations in their places — Orion sparkling above the wooded hill, the Pleiades milky above the pine spires, Cassiopeia above the house.

Here in Upper Turkeyfoot my universe converges. We do what we must.

January Catatonia

So much for the holidays.

The tree we cut from the hillside has been stripped of its glitter and lies now under the feeder as a windbreak for the birds.

The mailbox has been freed of its lights and stands unadorned and functional under the white pine that hangs over the dirt road. The mailman can now deliver those statements without catching his sleeve on the wire.

The painted, happy-faced, long-lashed, wooden flat people (snowmen are people, too) that please my wife and frighten the dog have been entombed in the attic for another 11 months.

No more checking lists twice. No more tape and scissors. No more clumsy events filled with concern and regret. No more exchanging viruses. Yes, the season of joy is over. The oven cools. Peace at last.

We can spend the evening as we like, going nowhere. We can sit all night, if we choose to do so, in our baggy sweats on the couch in front of the TV and breathe through our mouths.

We should be reading, we think, expanding our horizons, challenging our minds. But not now. Now we will just slouch and stare at three hours of pitches and comedies without coveting or laughing even once, benumbed.

Then the news, as always, of thievery and greed, of disaster and wreckage, mostly human. But we take it in stride now, exhausted. Not so a week or two ago.

A week or two ago when we had hoped briefly for a sane and just world, we found the news especially distressing. The only encouraging moment came in the report of a convicted murderer who unintentionally electrocuted himself with a homemade headset when, watching the tube just like a model citizen, he seated himself upon his stainless steel commode and gave himself the chair.

Otherwise, we found the news disturbing.

But wait. There was one other thing — a medical breakthrough which, although fit for television, seems unfit for print, this being a family newspaper read by kids and Republicans and Shouting Methodists and everybody. Let me just call it a cure for a male dysfunction, a pill taken in an unusual place from a device akin to a Pez dispenser.

It works by dissolving to open capillaries and promote blood flow thereby facilitating positive outcomes.

I use such language to show off my new skills in academese, acquired in a brief but torturous foray into the rarefied environment of higher education. Why, it even works on guys who have not facilitated positive outcomes for 40 years!

The anchorperson said the wonder drug remains effective for half an hour. This is wonderful news, indeed. I have one question: What do you do for the last 25 minutes?

Well, I suppose you can just try to relax and enjoy January, watch the days lengthen as the arctic purity of winter covers the land. Let us watch the snow pile up and listen to the wind howl under the eaves and collect ourselves.

Let us build up the fire and crawl under the old comforter. Let us open a good book. Let us close it and grab the remote and click on "Real Stories of the Highway Patrol."

It occurs to me that if the Highway Patrol were to kick in my door at this moment, they could seize much of the same stuff I see on the screen: guns (a shotgun fired annually on New Year's) and narcotics (left over from my last root canal) and $50 in cash (counting the penny tin).

I think they'd let me go. Not only do I wear a shirt, but my tree is down. Miscreants, I'll bet, leave it up through Ground Hog Day.

Seed Catalogs for Peace

I need a lift. Something to cheer me up. So I try a long walk, and it just makes my nose run.

I thought this Christmas I could recapture the joys of childhood. But I could not. I was foolish to think it possible. Yet I try every year, and fail, left with only the past and its regrets — inevitable, since there are no perfect lives.

Oh, I am in a black mood.

Before I return to the house and it's tired decorations, I stop at the mailbox. The mailman has been by; I see his tire tracks in the softening snow under the white pine. More debt, I'll bet.

Yet when I open the lid, the box is surprisingly empty. The mail order houses are wisely lying low, having thinned the northern forests, now that the credit card statements have been received. This is one of the reasons I need a lift. Call it "The Consumer's Blues."

But wait. In the dark recesses of the mailbox there is one catalog: The Gurney's Seed Catalog. Glory be!

Gladioli sprout on the cover. Currants hang heavy above ripe vegetables tumbling from a bushel basket. A little girl grins with an armful of gleaming tomatoes.

The timing couldn't be better. Gurney's is based in Yankton, South Dakota. In South Dakota they know a lot about mid-winter malaise.

My mood elevates. Hope exists. All things are possible. Flipping through the colorful pages in my living room with the icicles dripping down the window, I even believe I can grow watermelons.

Restraint. I need restraint. Impulse buying, after all, contributed to this funk. Facing a budget deficit, I must eliminate all nonessential vegetables.

I flip past cucumbers and rhubarb to potatoes. Potatoes are essential. I circle Kennebecs. Resistant to blight. Stores well. I'll take 30 sets. Make that 60. Oh, and better plant some russets, too. Early maturity. Best for baking. Yeah, and red Pontiacs. Good keepers. Great in heavy soil.

Kennebecs, russets, Pontiacs. There goes half the garden. But I'll still have room for corn (hybrid double delicious) and onions (yellow Ebenesers for early greens, Walla Wallas for sandwiches).

And tomatoes. Can't live without tomatoes. Improved Gurney Girls will fill the bill. Yes, and half a dozen sets of Subarctic Plenty, "world's earliest" with which to taunt the neighbors, early tomatoes being an indicator of your worth as a countryman.

This is great. I feel wonderful. Multiply this by the hundreds of thousands of catalogs Gurney's surely mailed out, and think of the benefit to society! A national cafard averted!

I'm onto something here. NATO should drop seed catalogs over Bosnia. Come spring, they could distribute seed packets and hoes. What Serb could resist summer squash? What Croat could remain bitter under the influence of purple-topped rutabaga? And by summer, if fighting breaks out, let them bombard each other with zucchini! Zuke 'em!

So, okay. Potatoes, onions, corn, tomatoes. Plus lettuce, although this year Black-seeded Simpson sounds frightening. And beets. A guy needs his iron. I feel healthier already.

I draw a sketch of where everything will go. I'll finish it off with a border of marigolds to keep out the rabbits and sunflowers which I'll leave up for the chickadees.

Between the rows I can squeeze in a mound of gourds which I'll dry and hang as bluebird houses. And if I till up another few feet, I could grow enough Japanese yellow hull-less popcorn to see me through next winter.

Forget nonessential. Dreams keep you sane.

A Tree Too Close

A pine tree grows close to the house. Too close.

Its roots have bellied out the fieldstone cellar wall, and I really should cut it down. But I won't. It brings me too much pleasure.

From just beyond the kitchen window it rises. I sit at the kitchen table as I write this, and I can see the texture of its bark, I can sense the roundness of its trunk shaded with the argent light of this overcast but bright afternoon.

Past the second story it goes, climbing higher than the roof peak. My son grew up in that upstairs room with the tree filling his window. He considered it a fire escape, vowing he would climb into its branches if he ever smelled smoke, or maybe even if he didn't.

Many mornings the tree was the first thing he'd see upon waking. Sometimes there were sparrows in it.

I know this tree. I have leaned a ladder against its side and with a saw tied to a line around my waist, climbed into its branches.

Old pines make easy climbing. Above the roof line I have climbed to cut away what lies against the shingles, and although the birds did not like it much, I have tarried there, my arms around the trunk, its bark sharp against my chest, its pitch sticky on my palms, to watch the sun go down.

It is snowing as I write, fine and windless, diffusing distance. The pine stands close, like an old friend.

From its lowest branch, level with the kitchen window, hang three feeders. Two I fill with sunflower seed, the third with thistle seed. After 25 years, the birds depend on me, especially in the snow.

Just now a jay has landed, frightening away the juncos and the purple finches feeding on the ground. The jay launches and leaves the feeder swinging. A nuthatch makes its way down the trunk. A downy woodpecker arrives to drill into the suet tied to the top of the branch.

Goldfinches in their brown winter feathers gobble thistle seed. Chickadees land in pairs. Cardinals wait in the white birch. I prefer the subtle, muted tones of the females, but what can compare to the males in the snow, as red as if they'd been invented?

Before I filled the feeders this morning, I stood beneath the tree and offered seed from my hand. A chickadee, after two passes, alighted on my thumb. I felt its nails on my flesh. It weighed nothing.

This tree's closeness to the house worries others. Strangers have commented on it. I suppose they wonder why I like it that way.

Ah, if only they knew I also welcome the mice in the cupboards, the squirrels in the attic, and the salamanders in the basement, surely they would think me eccentric. That wouldn't bother me. I'd think they don't know what they're missing.

Winter of our Discontents

So we're all snowed in together. This is big news all over the East. But not here in Upper Turkeyfoot. We're used to it here.

The phone has been ringing all evening. Neighbors call to make sure everybody's okay and to laugh about the hysterical reports coming out of the city where six inches has incited panic. Here, the picnic table under the pear tree has disappeared. Routine.

When the wind picks up, it'll take a bulldozer to reach us. I like that. According to the TV, everything's canceled. I like that , too—the force of nature slowing us down.

I click off the tube. I adjust the bindings to my snowshoes and listen to the wind against the house. It wasn't always so quiet.

I leaf through an old journal to remember what it was like when a storm trapped my two teenage children in the house with their old man. The following entries are from ten years ago to the day.

* * *

Mark Twain wrote that between the ages of 13 and 16, children should be kept in a barrel, and you should talk to them through the hole. From 16 to 19, he said, you should put in the cork.

I disagree. If I had a barrel, I'd have been in it myself. Dark, yes, but quiet. You see, I am paying the consequences for a musical Christmas (a mistake) — dueling stereos.

"Happy is the man whose time is his own."

I quoted this to the boy as he played "Pee Wee's Big Adventure" (another mistake) for the ninth time. He looked at me sideways.

"Time is your most valuable resource," I told him. "Don't waste it. Learn something."

"Oh, sure. Great. Fine," he said. (He has a penchant for sarcasm.) "Next you'll be telling me I should read."

"Ye gads, man! Read? Never would I suggest such sacrilege!" I said. (He gets it from me.)

The girl passed through the living room. This sighting was worth note, because she spends her time at home as a recluse, venturing out of her room only for provisions. But I know she's up there. I hear her woofers thump.

She slowed her pace and passed in front of the TV screen as if under water. The boy growled. She grinned. She has the the female talent for manipulating males. The boy exacts his revenge in the form of practical jokes, most often involving the toilet seat. I scramble to head off hostilities.

"I know," I said. "Let's all take a walk in the woods, have some hot chocolate, and watch the painting class on PBS!"

They exchange glances. For a moment I thought they actually communicated.

"Gee, Dad! Could we?" said the girl. "Could we really learn how to paint a happy little waterfall?" And she went back into hiding.

"Go ahead," I said, turning to the boy. "Grow up to be idiots."

"I know you are, but what am I?" he said.

I am happy to report that the children did not completely squander their extended vacation. The boy, blessed from birth with unique powers of emission, developed into a human rhythm section and can now provide a flawless beat for rap lyrics.

The girl, with the help of her grandfather, a former PIAA official, has mastered the rules of the National Football League. Her boyfriend is a fan. She anticipates conversing intelligently with him when he plants himself on my couch for the duration of the playoffs. That's okay. I'll just be glad for her presence.

According to the school calendar, Mid-Winter Break approaches. I am looking for a barrel.

* * *

Well, the house is quiet now. The snow piles up so high on the shrubbery I can't see out the windows. I think I'll call the kids.

You know, it is possible to miss bedlam.

Pitchers and Catchers

I never tire of watching snow fall against the woods. Good thing, because there is much left of winter.

It is dangerous, I think, to yearn for Spring. Better to seek out the pleasures of the day, to soak up the moment, to know the joys of the present.

Such philosophy comes easily, now that the water pipes have been repaired and school is back in session. Yet the signs of Spring are present, and they excite us.

Already we notice the lengthening of days. Already when the sun shines through a rare break in the cloud cover we hear the Spring "pee-vee" of the chickadees. Already we get press releases from the Pirates: Pitchers and catchers report on Feb. 16!

Oh, to be pitchers and catchers!

Oh, to be stretching your thighs in the Florida sunshine!

Oh, to be grinning with your pals and sharing anecdotes punctuated by the pop of the ball in the mitt!

Oh, to be trotting through the lush outfield grass, your off-season belly joggling under stylish double knit! ("I'm no athlete," John Kruk has said, "I'm a baseball player.")

Oh, to be my brother!

My brother, you see, goes to spring training. He's no team official, neither is he a pitcher nor a catcher, although he once struck out 18 in a seven-inning high school game, and the memory of warming him up still makes my hand ache. As they say, the boy could "bring it."

He had a tryout or two, my brother did. Went to Forbes Field and unleashed a few fastballs for the scouts. His elbow had been damaged by then, and it hurt him to throw. He went anyhow, just to say that he had.

Me, a spray-hitting second baseman who made up for my lack of power with slow-footedness, I never got past the 40-yard dash.

Thanks to an unusual thrashing motion (sometimes described as Groucho sprinting), I always looked faster than I was. The scouts would consult their watches and shake their heads. Once, they even asked me to run again, thinking their watches had failed simultaneously. But, no. I really was that slow.

So now each March my brother leaves behind the Maine winter and flies to Florida. He follows the Red Sox from Fort Myers to Bradenton (Pirates) to Clearwater (Phillies) to Lakeland (Tigers) to Sarasota (White Sox) to St. Petersburg (Cardinals) to Port Charlotte (Rangers) to Plant City (Reds) to Dunedin (Blue Jays) and back again. He exchanges greetings with the players. He tans.

Understand how much this means to him. My brother is a frugal man. This is a man who has driven the same station wagon 215,000 miles. This is a man who, as a boy, would hoard his candy corn and sell it to his prodigal brother at a penny per kernel.

Mom can tell you. "Jeff was always the creative one," she is wont to say. "But Jay always had more money."

And so it is.

I watch owls sail over the snowy fields and vanish into the mist like ghosts. Their mating has begun. I write and dream and look for signs of Spring. My brother flies into it and collects autographs.

Check Your Log Pile

Winter is half over. This is something I know. Groundhog Day, regardless of what they say in Punxsutawney, means we're halfway to Spring.

Do not despair. Halfway is good. No reason to rush it, no reason to be one winter closer to our last any earlier. Better to accept it. Best to revel in it.

"Be blown on by all winds," Thoreau said, and I believe in that. The Concord Transcendentalist led what seems to me to be an ideal life, a life of the mind.

One day a week he worked as a surveyor and spent the other six wandering the woods and fields and rivers, concerned with the cycles of the natural world and keeping the company of his own thoughts.

Thoreau could spend all day in his bean field hoeing and dreaming. He could do this because:

1. He lived simply, trying to have more by wanting less, confronting only the bare essentials of life.

2. His understanding neighbors allowed him to trespass. (His neighbors being writers, poets, and philosophers — the Emersons, the Hawthornes, the Channings, and the Alcotts.)

3. His father was knocking himself out in the family-owned pencil factory.

Thoreau believed it was more important (and more difficult) to spend the day attempting to create something true rather than something that would sell. Some citizens of Concord thought him a slacker. But the guy wrote, and writing is hard work.

Life, of course, was simpler then. It was a time of fewer choices. The point Thoreau made was that, regardless of number, choices exist, and that it was possible to live outside the consuming cycle of getting and spending, valuing time instead of money.

Owning little was a key.

"Keep you accounts on your thumbnail," he said.

He managed this by living with Mom and Dad or with friends. Even the cabin at Walden he built on Emerson's land.

Plus, he had these advantages:

1. He never had a wife.
2. He never had a dog.
3. He never had health insurance.

Nevertheless, I admire the guy. Inspired by that 19th Century eccentric, I spend what time I can outside, different drumming.

I love raw weather. I love the wind strong enough to lean on. I love the sleet that stings my cheeks. Never mind that Thoreau died of chronic bronchitis at 44.

And because I spend some time under the open sky, I know that winter is half over.

In the country on Candlemas Day (as it is known in Europe and in isolated pockets in these mountains inhabited by intellectuals) it is customary to check your wood pile and your hay. More than half remaining is a comfort.

There is also the old belief that the weather on February 2 will be the same kind of weather we will have for the rest winter.

This is something I am not so sure of, but if the sun shines on Sunday and the steam rises from the shed roof, I'll be less concerned about my wood pile.

Another reason I know winter is half gone is because I can watch golf on Saturdays instead of ice skating. I'm not sure when skating became so popular. There's been something "On Ice" every weekend. I'm just a simple country boy, and half the competition discomforts me, sort of the same feeling I get during a Matt scene on "Melrose Place," not that I really watch much TV when I should be reading Seneca.

There are more in ice skating championships, it seems, than in professional wrestling.

I might be on to something here: Wrestlemania Midget Tag-Team Cage Grudge Match of the Century On Ice. I'd watch that.

For a while anyway.

Then back to the Stoics.

Nature Never Fails Us

Dress warmly and come with me. I'll cure your cabin fever.

Yes, I know it's 40 degrees and raining. Against the blackened woods it falls upon the field like quicksilver. All the better. We'll have the world to ourselves.

Wear wool. It breathes and keeps you warm when wet. Something windproof overtop. See how the pines shake in the yard?

Here. Pull on this stocking cap and lift your hood. Ah, but how handsome you shall be with the rain upon your face.

Come on. The surface of the yard is sopping, yet feel the ice below, feel the hardness against our soles. The rain has washed away the snow and revealed in the field the tunnels of mice. Trace them to abandoned nests, mounds of grass lined with the finest blades where they feasted and cavorted beneath the drifts.

Sorry if I rattle on. Winter is a time for dreaming.

Andrew Wyeth, too, loves this season. You've seen his paintings, spare and moving. He speaks of the bone structure in the winter landscape.

"Something waits beneath it," Wyeth says. "The whole thing doesn't show."

Here at the edge of the woods, we know what he means. Under the thatched ruins of goldenrod await the green and jagged leaves of buttercup and strawberry. Hold still. In your hat I put a sprig of wintergreen, its red berry festive in the rain. It's good to see you smile.

Let us sit here on this log, backs to the wind. (Now you know why I brought squares of carpet padding.) Look around us while I take my journal from my pack. The rain has eased, and I want to make some notes. Tell me what you see.

The eye moves first to color: A fern at our feet flattened by the weight of winter and half covered with oak leaves — so many fall after the snow begins; the verdigris of lichen spotting the trunk of a massive oak; the moss we sit on; pluck a bit while I dig for the hand lens. Look how its fronds divide and divide again, how it duplicates itself in miniature. See even the lichen's graceful leaves.

Rain taps on the page, dissolving my scrawled letters into bursts very much the shapes of lichen. So much in nature takes the shape of leaves.

As we sit, the more subtle pleasures show themselves. We have only to wait.

On the umber weave of the leaf mat we discover the signs of a rabbit, then 20 feet away, the rabbit herself, stoic and staring, the wild gleam of life in her black eye.

In budded twigs around us hang raindrops, small hemispheres of sky with the world inverted in each one. Treetops sway over us in quiet wind, yet hear it screaming on the wooded hilltops. The sky is gray and close and moving fast.

The day belongs to us.

We imagine our neighbors ensconced in their living rooms, televisions on, feeling caged and remarking to each other, if at all, upon this "dreary day." We nearly did the same.

We are our own jailers.

Steadying in the Thaw

You say you miss our walks, feeling there is nothing stable in this world. Let us go then, while the water runs.

You say you are perplexed by doubts and fancies. You say, as Keats complained, that uproar is your only music. Let us go then, while the ground softens and the fog thickens.

Go ahead, laugh — it pleases me — laugh at my elbow sticking through my sweater. The moths know where it hangs, and it has fed many generations in 20 years on the same nail in the cellarway. But it keeps me warm just the same, and the holes make me happy. Yes, I am easily amused. That is a privilege of simple living.

Today is made for wool — a light and steady rain, 35 degrees. Wool keeps us warm when wet, and nothing breathes as well. It adapts to the day and what we do with it. So let us walk, and let the day itself fill that void which clamor cannot reach. We immerse ourselves in now.

We step outside. Though it is cold and mizzling, the sparrows sing as if it were summer. Though overcast and wet, the air has brightened some since morning, and the birds tell us the rain will end soon. The day is raw and elemental, its beauty subtle. This kind of mid-winter day is an acquired taste, like single malts, appreciated best by those who like a bit of bite and burn.

The yard around the house shows green and yellow, vivid and startling after weeks of snowcover. But the fields and woods remain white. The warmth of human habitation penetrates the ground. We see the evidence only on days as rarefied as this.

We frighten doves out of the hemlocks as we walk the yard. What had been for days a solid dome of gray gains definition now, and we see movement in the sky at last. Rain shines in the white pine — at the tip of each needle, a single, brilliant drop.

Just yesterday morning when we stepped outside, a miscreant wind from the northeast stole the warmth from our bodies and scattered it across the snow crust, rolled it under the splitrail fence and bounced it in shards over the ice in the woods, tumbling with the hulls of birch seeds emptied by small and desperate winter birds exhausting their stores.

Yet today they sing, and the wind has no threat in it, only promise. The rain deepens the ochers and siennas of the weeds standing above the ice, and the ruddiness of buds hangs in the crowns of trees.

We begin to feel it. Steadiness returns. Away from the churnings of unmitigated greed, we find a starting place.

We need but a few points from which to build our day, as the the spider builds its web. We have doves exploding from the hemlocks. We have rain hanging in the pines. We have a start.

When we taste the weather every day, remain still under the sky and let nature show herself, infusing us with the constancy of cycles, with the slow undulations of the seasons, with the rhythms of existence, our perplexities lose their sting.

Removed from culture, we build the day around what's real, starting with our own intelligence and with our hearts, spinning a line to the doves and to the drops to build ourselves.

You spoke of Keats. This is the process he called "Soulmaking." We begin with our intelligence and our hearts, he believed, and as the world acts upon us and we react to it, we form our identities. Perplexity fashions our souls.

Keats knew quite young what it takes most of us twice as long to learn: That we cannot count on happiness; that it is enough to be free from pain; that nothing startles beyond the present moment.

If a sparrow comes to our window, he said, we should take part in its existence, and pick about the gravel. Yes, Keats was a hopeless romantic. But so are we, underneath it all.

Buoyed by an intelligent naivete, we walk the sopping yard. Runoff boils up from a mole hole in a small artesian well, depositing topsoil in tiny alluvial plains. The earth gurgles and ticks.

Alone, wearing ragged sweaters in the rain, our thoughts are our own. We abandon mimicry. We are ourselves.

Surely, there is stability in that.

Heeby-Jeebies

I'm shaken. Call it the "inside willies."

This happens when I'm cooped up too long. Boxed is what I am, crated like a chicken on its way to market. It's unnatural.

A farmer I know claims any place without cows or trees makes him nervous. I understand that, except I love the desert, too. All that open space, all those long views. In fact, for the same reasons and with the right gear, I believe I'd love Siberia.

Now that I've typed that here in front of me where I can analyze it, it seems what I love is solitude. What I love is quiet.

I'll treat myself today. The morning is cold and bright. I'll cross the frosted field and build a fire in the cabin in the woods. The sun rises behind the trees as I write.

Yes. I will cut firewood with the bow saw. I will wrap myself in wool and sit in the rocker on the porch. Today my news will be of buds swelling and birds arriving. I will know the weather by the clouds and wind, by the feel of the open air. I encourage you to do the same.

Escapism, you say? Well, that is my privilege, and I will take it.

Daydreaming while society crumbles, you charge? Perhaps, but if we scour the world for signs of the Apocalypse, we are sure to find them. Portents of Armageddon have always existed.

Today, at this moment, I cannot end suffering, insure justice, save the Earth. The best I can do is remove myself from the whir for an hour, regain my faith in cycles, renew my reverence for all things natural, and move on with hope restored.

Is it naive to think the world would be a saner place if we all did that? Very well then, I am naive.

All this talk about the Millennium spooks us. Atavistic instincts aroused, we look for omens. We are more primitive than we had thought.

Every event gains importance. No sooner has my heart rate slowed from the near-miss of Hyakutake, than here came Hale-Bopp. Last March I stood astonished in a frigid wind; the comet's tail, away from city lights, covered a third of the night sky, bisecting the Big Dipper. That's close, I thought, real close. If it were headed straight for Upper Turkeyfoot, would they tell me? Hey, I've seen "X-Files."

I sign on to the Internet and learn that leaders of the free world are falling down.

Israeli President Ezer Weizman stumbled out of a helicopter fracturing his wrist and thigh. President Clinton caught a heel on Greg Norman's staircase at 1:20 a.m. in West Palm Beach and ripped up his knee.

Surely there's a verse in Revelations about this.

And that's just the beginning. The swallows have come back to Capistrano four days early.

I pick up the newspaper and learn skunks are massing in Ebensburg. What does this mean? Do we head for the bunkers?

I flip on the tube. "Gruesome Discovery" flashes across the bottom of the screen. "Details on Action News at Noon."

No thanks. I've heard and seen enough for today. I'm sure I'll miss graphic descriptions of the President's tendons and bones, but we've already seen Johnson's stitches, Nixon's veins, and an artist's conception of Reagan's large colon. We've witnessed Carter swoon and Bush heave.

I think I'd prefer to return to the days of misinformation, like when Grover Cleveland's mouth cancer was passed off as a toothache.

It is possible to know too much. I'm off to the woods. Leave a message.

Considering Chickens

The snow slid off the garage roof in one soft sheet Saturday, and I began to expect Spring. But while my neighbors are flipping through their seed catalogs, I'm dreaming about chickens.

I used to have chickens, and I'd like to have them again. The old coop is still there. I stomped through the slush to check it out.

I use it now as a shed for the perennial garden. Rakes and hoes and little shovels hang inside, but to me it seems empty. I liked it better when it was full of squawking and warm eggs and feathered commotion.

The mice have been busy, I see. Their excavations follow the perimeter of the earthen floor which still bears signs of the birds that once roosted here.

This is rich dirt. If I were to rip off the roof and plant tomatoes, they would grow taller than the walls and become the talk of Upper Turkeyfoot. I would probably get my picture in Let's Talk Turkey (the local paper), my tomatoes and me, just like the guy who last summer grew a squash resembling Richard Nixon.

The roosts could be easily repaired and the laying boxes are good. I had insulated the coop years ago with sheets of beaded foam which the chickens promptly ate. I worried for their health then, but they seemed to thrive on it. Chickens are hearty creatures. I long for clucking.

Inspired, I called around. I'm an impulse buyer, and though I've never before purchased chickens with my MasterCard, I wanted to try. But I didn't have much luck.

There are just two listings in our Yellow Pages under "Poultry-Whsle." At Bird Poultry Co. nobody answered. And at Oaks Poultry, Inc., the woman laughed when I asked for pullets.

"You mean freshly dressed?" she asked.

"No," I said. "I mean, you know, peeps."

"Oh my!" she said. "We haven't been live for 35 years."

"Sometimes it seems as if it's been awhile for me, too," I said, and our conversation took on a more philosophical tone.

Maybe I'll drive over the mountain into Amish country as I did the last time I stocked the coop. The Amish are friendly folk, and I pulled into the first rocky lane I saw where the man stood waving in the yard.

"Can I buy some chickens from you?" I asked.

"You can if you want to," he said, scratching under his beard. The Amish have a way of looking at me that makes me uneasy. I see myself for a moment through their eyes, and I seem ridiculous.

"Great," I said. "Which ones?"

"The ones you can catch," he said.

His children and his dogs were a big help. We developed a system of trapping them under the corn crib. We had a grand time.

These chickens were a rough bunch. Upon release, they strutted about the yard fiery-eyed and hook-beaked and sharp-spurred, croaking and looking for a fight. The cats fled. Finding no takers, they flailed away at each other for a few minutes, established a pecking order, and settled down to rule their domain.

They laid clutches of small, brown eggs in the hayfield. The roosters crowed every time the sun reappeared from behind a cloud. The hens, trailing a line of speckled chicks, snapped up every shoot in the vegetable garden. I miss chickens.

The complexities of life rendered this place chickenless. For a time I had my priorities mixed up—too much to do, too long in town, too rushed to scatter feed and gather eggs and chase away the weasels.

Days too busy for chickens, it seems to me now, are days squandered.

Where We Find It

A friend bought an acre in the tropics.

St. John, Virgin Islands. On a hillside. Palms riffling above an emerald sea. Says he'll build: Mediterranean. Says he wants to do it right. He vacationed there last winter, and he speaks of the island with reverence.

"Every morning, when you open your eyes," he says, "you're amazed all over again."

I never thought I'd know any one with an acre in the West Indies. I shared this astonishing news with other friends over lunch.

"You know Barry, the guy that owns that employment agency?" I said, plucking fuzz balls from the edges of my trouser pockets.

They nodded without looking up from their salads.

"He just bought an acre in the Virgin Islands!" I said.

"No kidding?" they said.

"Yeah," I said." He says when you open your eyes every morning, you're amazed."

And, to the person, they responded with something like:

"True, but I prefer sunsets in the Keys."

...or the beaches of Aculpulco.

...or the restaurants of Paris.

...or the blondes of Scandinavia.

One guy just grinned and waved a pamphlet that said "St. Croix" on the front.

"I can't wait," he said.

One week they're munching croutons from a plastic plate and the next they're snorkeling in the Caribbean.

When did all of this happen, and where was I?

And where am I?

I took a morning walk the next day and thought about it, empty with want.

Frost sparkled in the shaded field beside the wood as the sun climbed white into the treetops and fog receded into the hollow. The scree and chatter of awakening birds filled the woods. The frost began to melt, dripping, dripping on the leaf mat.

Light clung silver to the branches, thickening the hillside into a gauze of gleaming twigs and crystal beads, fiery prisms blazing ice blue and red and golden green.

Crows organized their day against the ringing blue. Steam rose from the cabin roof. The hollow echoed with the hammering of a woodpecker.

While I basked in the sun on the cabin porch, by that heat and that twitter, I was absolved from longing.

Nature did its work on me. I knew my life to be as fleeting as the frost, a white shadow existing but a moment as the sun swings 'round.

What brings peace to my existence, if I can't find it here, would be fruitless to search for elsewhere.

What I want surrounds me. All I have to do is open my eyes, and be amazed.

Late Winter Rant

Blame it on seasonal dysfunction if you like, but I'm in a foul mood.

This morning I was fine. I began the day with confidence, charged with coffee, convinced this would be a day of great accomplishment. The snow was gone, the grass wet. Yes, today I would experience genius, create beauty, hit a four-iron straight and true.

Then I opened the mail. The yellow envelope. I should have known. A credit collection service claims I owe $14.79 for an insurance policy on a car I sold before the policy expired. The insurance company, in fact, owes me.

For three months I have been making phone calls and writing letters. Yet here it is again, this yellow letter. I have fallen into a computer somewhere in Massachusetts, and I can't get up.

This is scary stuff. The letter threatens me with words like "sheriff" and "seven years under federal law" and, the most frightening of all, "The Internal Revenue Service."

I spring into action. I pick up the phone. It is Sunday. Nobody answers. I'll bet they're all in church, dropping $14.79 into the collection plate.

O'Brien is upset. He needs to calm down. Sometimes it helps him when he refers to himself in the third person.

O'Brien goes outside. With a four iron. He swings. The ball hits the power line, bounces high off the road, and into the pond. He sees none of this. He is stumbling into the house to flush the mud from his eyes. O'Brien is not so good at golf.

Standing under the inverted eye cup, he realizes he should take his own advice. A few days earlier he had stood before high school students and quoted Emerson.

Genius resides in each of us, he said, if only we take the time to listen to ourselves. He encouraged them to sit quietly outside for half an hour, to open themselves to the world at their feet, to hear their own thoughts.

He daubs his eyes, blows his nose, and does just that.

It works.

I sit coatless beside the pond. This is the joy of March, to one day have your feet in snow, and the next to bask in the sun beside raveling water.

Hemlock needles form a raft against the bank, shaped by the wind into tight patterns of which the hand is incapable. When I bend to plug a hole bored by crayfish, water boatmen flee, rowing deep into the cold water.

A leopard frog, dark with cold, kicks away from the shallows. How good the flexing must feel after months in the muck. Tadpoles flutter off. A pair of song sparrows clatter about in the cattails. They seem to be here for the same reason as my own, for the pure pleasure of warmth and open water.

The log on which I sit brims with life, a thousand tiny movements, enlivened by the sun and south wind. A small perch nips at the surface, testing the margin of its world.

A tadpole floats on jade, warming; a bubble escapes from its mouth, and it swims straight down, exposing its pale belly when I move.

The sparrows sing. The light reflects in ripples on undersides of ash limbs. I feel the rhythm, the pulse of life, the same that runs in me.

It is a good day for us all.

Running in Snow

Running is a solitary enterprise, like writing. But you can come this time.

With only our eyes and cheekbones exposed, we step onto the back porch, our breath freezing. Icicles hang from the eaves. Crows call. 12 degrees.

A little skip (a habit we've developed over the years) and we're off. We break through drifts in the yard to reach the road. The thin snow crust breaks into polygons.

We run in the tire tracks of a neighbor's truck whose coming and going has kept the road from filling up where the wind blows freely across the open fields.

Rows of corn stubble recede into valley. The sun shines on the other side, beams radiating from behind a cloud. How we love the line of the hilltop against the sky, the rise and fall of the earth in the simplified landscape of winter.

We move through the blue-and-gold of early evening. Blue shadows fill the hollows. Sunlight limns the ridges of the drifts.

We cross the hard road and wave at neighbors looking through their picture window. A flock of killdeers, just arrived, race low over this cornfield where we always see them first.

One mile now. We fall into our rhythm, we find our pace. I have run this route so often, I know the mullein that stands desiccated in the snowbank; I have noted its sprouting and its growth, its flowering and maturing to seed. As much as I enjoy the beauties of winter, it will be good to see its wooly leaves again.

Barns are small red blocks on the distant hills. Here at this field returning to woods, in not too many weeks we can stop and pick strawberries, stain our fingers and taste the wildness.

Down the hill we shorten our stride, wary of ice. When we see the brick farmhouse through bare oaks, we turn around. Sunlight spreads toward us from the middle distance. We measure our stride against our own tracks.

How vivid the few colors that exist amid the bleached expanse of snow and sky — the orange tractor under a mantle of snow, the red barns, the green forage wagon pulled halfway out of shed.

The wind blows hard against us. Snow snakes across the road like smoke. A crow flies close, gaining lift from the wind that slows us. He keeps his distance, beyond a stone's throw, a smart and sharp-eyed bird.

We turn the bend and run directly toward the sun. Ice particles have formed around our hoods like frost around the freezer door.

Up the dirt road we go, dunes of snow between us and the snow fence stretched and sagging by a season's wind.

We count squirrel nests high in the treetops among the grapevines, their roofs covered with snow, the squirrels hidden within.

We top the last hill and head for home. Our speed increases. We feel what horses feel when they sense their return to their stable. With the sun in eyes and our legs feeling strong, we turn it up a notch for the last hundred yards.

And we stop. And we hear the crows again. And we hear our hearts. We walk with our faces turned skyward. Right now we feel attuned to the natural world, blended with the elements, the sun on our faces, the steam rising from our flesh, standing on the earth, under the sky, hurtling through the void.

Soon we will cool down and must head for the room and the fire lest we catch a chill. But right now, we know exhilaration. It lasts only a moment. Everything does.

The Soul in the Machine

This column is being written on a manual typewriter. So if it reads a little looser, that's the reason. If it runs a little longer, if it flows a little smoother, that's the reason. To me, it feels fine.

No spell checker, no pathetic thesaurus, no print preview. No cathode rays, no spinning fans, no heat — unless you consider the heat generated by the muscles in my forearms. Ah, the exercise of mind and body.

No grammar checker, no search and replace. None of that. Word processing remains solely a function of the head.

Only me and my fingers and this heavy, old, thundering, archaic, marvelous machine, still functioning, still connecting my mind to yours despite years of neglect, despite the nest of shredded paper and insulation I plucked from its innards, despite the nut hulls and the dust; it does its job and feels natural to me, right for the rhythms of my thoughts, and it pleases me to see the words appear.

And when I finish this page (I have remembered just now to give the knob a spin and make a mark an inch above the bottom), when I finish this page I can lay it on the desk, I can read continuously from start to stuck. No continuous scrolling, no page up or page down, no limit to the lines I can absorb by looking. I can cover the floor if I wish. Oh, I am ecstatic.

(MORE)

Forgive my nostalgia. You see, this is how I learned, encouraged by the flying strikers, thrilled by the advancing ribbon when the words came, the force of an idea notable by its blackness, ending a sentence with a period that pierced the page, the rubber roller pocked with thoughts completed.

The feel of it. The feel of it more sensual than the nifty extended keyboard wired to my computer with those keys I never use (esc, F1-F15, and the entire calculator block), a keyboard for which I have never developed the delicate touch. My hands know only the deep, strong strokes of the manual. Using old knowledge again gives me the satisfaction of, say, splitting wood — the swing of the axe, the pop of the log, the thunk of the blade in the stump, period. Yes, there is a physical pleasure this old Royal provides, tied to the masculine perhaps, and real.

I learned to write in a newsroom. I learned from a pro, a third-generation newsman, with his wide lapels and his hair slicked back and parted in the middle, an editor of the classic style, full of cynicism and bourbon. I'd return from assignment, drape my coat over the back of the chair, open my notebook, and I'd write. I had to.

"No Pulitzer tonight," he'd say, tapping his leather soles on the tile under his desk and glancing at the clock. "Just make it right."

The newsroom was a busy place, and loud; reporters shouting back and forth, phones ringing, a din of creation, a concussion of writing, the typewriters clacking and dinging and sometimes screeching as a page was yanked from the carriage, crumpled and tossed in disgust, a catharsis lacking in Microsoft Word.

(MORE)

I mean, look at this machine, weighty and substantial, maybe even ponderous, sturdy enough to lean on. With its chrome levers and releases, its calibrated bars, powerful springs, and the recurve of the key arms under my fingers, it is a combination of the brutish and the beautiful.

And look at this page. Hard copy. Feel it between thumb and forefinger, see the m'ed-out characters and the overstrikes and the tendrils of emendation in my own hand. Before me is not only the finished work, but the evidence of craftsmanship (such as it is) as well, the trail of the creative process. Oh, I have missed that.

I love to see the ribbon jump and hear the ding and throw the carriage back with a satisfying clunk. This old workhorse I bought for $25 from the publisher of the small town newspaper after they plugged in Selectrics. I never really liked the ball.

Years ago I lugged it into the woods and set it up in the cabin on the swing-up shelf of the old desk, spring-loaded and counter-weighted. They were made for each other.

Today, on an impulse, I swung out the shelf and left the portable computer in its case. I am happy to be typing again. Like any machine worth the effort, it was designed for hard service and is the better for it — the gears and joints freeing themselves as I go. An old romance has been rekindled. Thanks for indulging me. I close traditionally.

-30-

Last snow

Sit with me awhile. I've built a fire inside the cabin. Let us sit on the porch a minute and watch the snow fall against the dark trees, fine and slow.

Pull up that chair with its wicker unraveling. Wrap yourself in this wool blanket. Yes, yes, you have work to do. It shows.

But just sit for a minute, away from the jangling phone, away from ambition. Just stop maneuvering long enough to know where you are in this world. Just sit on this porch on this wooded hillside with your breath before you, and enjoy the silence.

Last night's snow fleeces every limb and twig, thickening the woods. The wind is gently rising, and clots of snow are falling with a whump, pocking the forest floor where the snow lies knee deep.

It is warm — mid-thirties, I'll bet — and the tree trunks are dark with melt. Never has the woods looked more black-and-white.

The chickadees have found the seed. It never takes them long. Wilder than the ones around the house, they must judge us benign before they'll eat. Look how they come 'round the corner to inspect us. Hear their wings buffeting the damp air. See the gleam in their black eyes.

The titmice are arriving, too; how they squawk as they dip toward us. A jay screams in the maple thicket. News of food travels quickly.

The birds feast now, darting in, grabbing a seed in their beaks and flying off, the titmice raising their crests, the nuthatches alighting on the post, hopping down to the sunflower seed scattered on the deck, then back up the post for takeoff. Hear their nails scrape against the oak.

The gray squirrel whose tracks we see at our feet scampers across the side of the cabin. The same colors as the weathered chestnut siding to which he clings, he looks mussed, as if he just awoke. Squirrels do not hibernate, but sleep a lot in winter, nevertheless.

I am sorry. I talk too much. Just listen.

What is it? Clients will be calling, you say? Shh. They will find you soon enough. The GNP will recover from your absence; the business world will survive for an hour or two without you.

And besides, it is a fool's life, as Thoreau believed we will discover at the end of it. Who but a fool, he asked, would strive for more than life's necessities when he could instead be considering the quality of the day.

So sit here among wing beats and say nothing. Take notice of what dwells within these woods, within you. Society, upon your return, will be as frantic as you left it. Ah, but you may not be. Just sit.

Sometimes I think we are too much in motion. The automobile and our reliance upon it causes us to dread winter. Yet if we lived slower, more rooted lives, we would find snow storms only astonishing.

Winter, more than any other season, forces us to examine our lives. We realize how far we live from the natural world, and what that does to us. Better we should observe the hours of the universe, not of the cars.

Much is about to happen. Soon we will see robins. It won't be long. Catkins will swell, and the first warm rain will start the peepers singing. Frogs will dig themselves out of the mud, and maples will bloom. Blackbirds will chortle atop fence posts, and geese will trumpet in the sky. All this in a matter of days.

This snow could be our last. Let us savor it.

I shall be quiet, finally.

Listen.